I0825726

TRUE STORIES
of Elmira, New York
Volume 4

By Diane Janowski & James Hare

This book is a selection of their freelance articles
in the Elmira *Star-Gazette*

True Stories of Elmira, New York, Volume 4

ISBN: 978-1-950822-06-5

Printed in the United States of America

First Edition

Cover image: Eldridge Park Casino and Lake, circa 1880. Albumin photograph by Elisha Van Aken. Courtesy of the Barnes Library.

Dedicated to
Aaron and Danielle, and grandson Noah
Matt and Amanda, and grandson Shea

Table of Contents

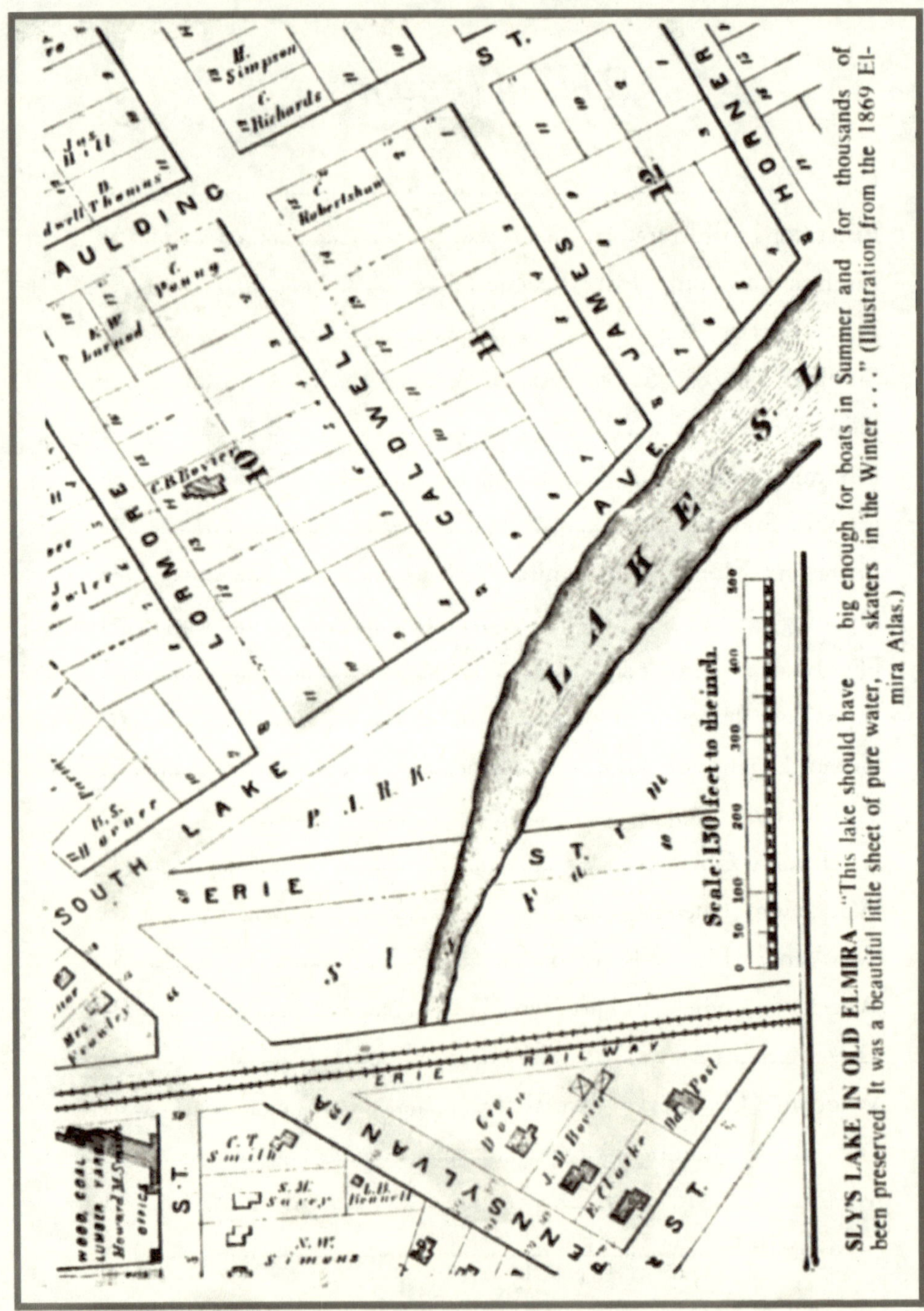

1869 map in the April 26, 1953 *Star-Gazette* depicting the area of Lake Sly.

Lake Sly

By Diane Janowski

As you drive on the Clemens Center Parkway just south of Pennsylvania Avenue you see an exit for Lake Avenue. Then you think, "What lake? There is no lake around here." Today's Lake Avenue was named for Lake Sly of 150 years ago.

Lake Sly, or sometimes Sly's Pond, was originally part of a relay of water and a continuous creek that bulged out at the pond. There were two, or sometimes three ponds depending on the weather or season connected by a twin stream that ran down to Miller's Pond. The main section of the lake was about 1,800-feet long and 150-feet wide. Youngsters caught frogs, carp, bull heads, and sunfish. The beautiful ice in winter made for wonderful ice skating.

Former county historian Clark Wilcox in 1953 remembered, "Between Hudson and Partridge Streets was a race course park. A large hotel called the Park Hotel accommodated the racing people and visitors. A sparkling little brook had its rise near this park and flowed east along the north side of Partridge Street. This was a beautiful little sheet of pure water, big enough for boats in summer, and for thousands of skaters in the winter."

Lake Sly was gradually filled in starting in 1888, but that was not fast enough for the locals. According to the *Star-Gazette* on April 10, 1895 city health inspectors were called to the lake to address the garbage and toxins in the water. At the end of Brand Street, hundreds of dead carp lined the shore, evidently poisoned by the water. The largest fish weighed 16 pounds and was longer than 3 feet. Four barrels of dead fish weighing more than 750 pounds were carted to a farm south of the city limits.

The city continued filling the lake. The *Star-Gazette* on June 4, 1901 said, "Many improvements are being made. [The] unsightly place is being filled in, and walks repaired...It is now a matter of only a few years when this pond will be wholly eliminated. It is growing smaller year by year and will soon be but a possible memory to the residents."

By 1904, the lake had no inlets or outlets. Water only gathered in the spring and was stagnant until it dried up. It was a handy place to throw rubbish. Things, or people that went missing were alleged to be at the bottom of the pond.

In 1907, the city posted signs not to dump refuse there. In 1911, the area was leveled off and flattened. In 1912, neighbors asked the board of public works to "rid the neighborhood of an old eyesore."

The situation grew worse before it got better. Not everyone in 1915 had indoor plumbing yet, and what had been dumped into the lake in earlier years, now was dumped in the filled-in lake area. Sewage, rubbish, rotted vegetable matter, and ashes were a common sight. Neighbors believed the local mosquitoes had malaria. The health inspectors were ordered to do a better job patrolling the "dumping grounds" at Lake Sly. Health inspectors did report that since the last board meeting, more than half of the 45 cases of diphtheria, scarlet fever, tuberculosis, and measles had been reported in the Brand Street area.

In 1916 the plot was taken over by the city from Charles A. Pulford, owner of the land. The city planned to improve the plot and establish a park there. By 1921, the area was being called Sly Park. On June 20, 1921 the Omaha Giants came to play the Elmira Has Beens in the first city league baseball game held there.

On June 27, 1925, six community tennis courts opened on the site of the former lake with an exhibition game featuring American tennis legend Clifford Marsh and local athlete Strang Curtis. Marsh defeated Curtis in two straight sets, 6-0 and 6-1. The opening of these tennis courts spiked a huge increase in sales of tennis equipment at local sporting goods stores. In the winters the courts were used as skating rinks. The city kept good care of the tennis courts. Every spring new clay dressings were leveled. Tennis leagues provided good exercise for Elmirans.

The brand new clay tennis courts at Sly Park on June 13, 1927. Image from the *Star-Gazette*.

By 1947, talks were underway to add lighting to Sly Park. In 1948 blacktop surfaces were laid on two of the six tennis courts.

The city demolished the Sly Park tennis courts in 1964. The loss of courts marked the end of clay courts in Elmira. The city claimed it was too expensive to maintain the clay ones. Brand Park eventually had new blacktop courts added.

By 1969 the park had fallen into disrepair, and the 1972 flood did not help matters. It received some grant money in 1977. Today in the park are a few swings, benches, and a picnic area were the tennis courts once received great attention.

So, the next time you pass the Lake Avenue exit, think of dear old Lake Sly.

Sources:

Star-Gazette (Elmira, New York) 26 Apr 1953, Sun Page 36
Star-Gazette (Elmira, New York) 21 Dec 1954, Tue Page 17
Star-Gazette (Elmira, New York) 17 Apr 1966, Sun Page 7
Star-Gazette (Elmira, New York) 05 Dec 1954, Sun Page 34
Star-Gazette (Elmira, New York) 10 Apr 1895, Wed Page 5
Star-Gazette (Elmira, New York) 04 Jun 1901, Tue Page 5
Star-Gazette (Elmira, New York) 23 Dec 1916, Sat Page 3
Star-Gazette (Elmira, New York) 04 Jun 1912, Tue Page 3
Star-Gazette (Elmira, New York) 13 May 1907, Mon Page 2
Star-Gazette (Elmira, New York) 20 Apr 1911, Thu Page 7
Star-Gazette (Elmira, New York) 04 Sep 1920, Sat Page 14
Star-Gazette (Elmira, New York) 25 Aug 1904, Thu Page 8
Star-Gazette (Elmira, New York) 22 May 1925, Fri Page 17
Star-Gazette (Elmira, New York) 23 Sep 1925, Wed Page 7
Star-Gazette (Elmira, New York) 20 Jun 1925, Sat Page 8
Star-Gazette (Elmira, New York) 06 May 1936, Wed Page 15
Star-Gazette (Elmira, New York) 09 Dec 1947, Tue Page 18
Star-Gazette (Elmira, New York) 17 May 1964, Sun Page 42

Executions in Elmira

By James Hare

"The neighborhood of the courthouse and jail was populated by a crowd of persons, who could not possibly see anything but outside brick and stone walls, but who could imagine a good deal…A company of military (the 30th Separate) luckily not disbanded by Governor Cornell guarded the surroundings of the jail…." reported the *Sunday Morning Tidings* of January 8, 1882.

The crowd had gathered for the public hanging of Joseph Abbott on Friday, January 6 at the Chemung County Jail. Abbott was an inmate of the Elmira Reformatory. According to the late Sheriff Charles Houper, writing for the *Chemung Historical Journal* in June, 1990, "During a fight with another inmate, George Reed, who struck him first, allegedly Abbott took an iron pipe and beat Reed to death. Because it wasn't premeditated, he should have been found guilty of second degree murder. However he was ultimately found guilty of first degree murder." The case aroused much debate and discussion, not only about guilt or innocence but the whole concept of execution by hanging.

Reporters from as far away as Chicago came to cover his trial Houper noted. News coverage of the actual execution was detailed with a picture of the gallows included. On the morning of the event, Sheriff Levi D. Little, at the prisoner's request read the death warrant in the cell instead of at the gallows. Abbott said he wanted it done where it was warm. "He said he had been so long indoors that he didn't want to stand in the cold shivering, listening to anything… he wanted the outside business done as soon as possible." When the procession reached the gallows, the newspaper reported that, "Abbott took his place directly beneath the rope, without direction, knowing intuitively what was required…before anything was done, he turned to the Sheriff and said—'Sheriff I want to say a few words to this crowd.'

'All right' said the officer.

Taking a step forward, Abbott said distinctly, 'Gentlemen, you witness in my death, a terrible injustice.' Then to the Sheriff, 'I'm ready.'

The newspaper went on to explain in great detail, the adjusting of the noose, the placement of the cap, the severing of the cord, and the resulting jerk of the body in the air, "with a suddenness that was as startling as it was effective." Unfortunately, it was not effective. Abbott's neck was not broken as planned and it was sixteen minutes later that he was pronounced dead by strangulation and dropped into his coffin.

The *Sunday Morning Tidings* concluded the article noting that, "thus endeth the third ghostly tragedy in Chemung County and the third victim of the same deadly gallows."

In the last half of the 19th century there were five people sentenced to die in Chemung County. Sheriff Houper wrote that, "the first individual escaped and was never heard from again. The last individual won a change of venue and he ended up in Broome County where he met the fate he should have received here."

Prior to the execution of Joseph Abbot, Henry Gardner was executed for murder on March 1, 1867 and Peter H. Penwell met his fate on July 20, 1877.

On March 16, 1865, the body of Amassa Mulock was found, "on the top of the high hills in the woods to the northwest of Judge Gray's residence and back of the Sly farm…the body was well preserved, having been thoroughly frozen, but the head had been crushed in by blows from a musket, the broken stock still lying by his side…" Mulock was described as an "aged, peculiar and industrious man, familiarly known as the 'old tree doctor' having been employed the previous summer in clearing shade trees along our principal streets of the destructive borer." At the time of his disappearance he had two or three hundred dollars with him and two watches according to the Elmira *Daily Advertiser* of March 2, 1867.

His body was discovered by two soldiers from the 12th Regulars stationed at Barracks 3 guarding Confederate prisoners. The murderer was an-

Preparations for Hanging Abbott.

ELMIRA, N. Y. Jan. 2.—Preparations have already been begun at the jail for the execution of Joseph Abbott, the day fixed for carrying out the sentence being on Friday next. The execution will take place in the north jail yard, a small enclosure perhaps fifty feet east and west and twenty feet north and south, surrounded by a high brick wall. This enclosure is now being roofed over. The approach to it is from the northwest tower of the jail building by means of a narrow doorway.

The rope to be used is one with which Penwell was hanged in 1877. It is small in size but is made of the best shoemakers thread, and has been tested with a weight of more than five hundred pounds. It cost Sheriff Beers $15 and was manufactured in Rochester.

Abbott still maintains his spirits, sleeps and eats well and shows no signs at all of breaking up. He has said before that there is no use in whimpering.

Image from The *Daily News,* Lebanon, Pennsylvania, Tuesday, January 3, 1882, page 1

other soldier, Henry E. Gardner. He had been missing from camp on the day of the murder. Upon his return, his gun was unaccounted for and previously he had no watch and had attempted to borrow money. The news paper noted that after Mulock's disappearance Gardner was "well supplied with currency and extravagant and profuse in his expenditures...showing off his watches."

Gardner would be arrested, tried, convicted and sentenced to hang on March 1, 1867. He was 23 years of age. His last words were "Liquor is the ruination of any man." This would be the first execution for murder in Chemung County. The March 2 *Advertiser* noted the characteristics of the "morbid curiousity" aroused by the hanging. "It drew men, women and children from the farthest confines of the county—it thronged the streets in the morning—crowded the avenues to the Court House on all sides at noon—jostled and jammed pushed and squeezed...All this merely to get a view of the enclosure within which a fellow mortal was appointed to die..." Those inside the walls seemed less curious, "yet even here, a desire to secure 'a bit of the rope' exhibited a similar trait of humanity."

The headline for the *Daily Advertiser* on March 12, 1877 told the story of the second hanging in Elmira: "An Old Man Kills His Wife, Jealousy The Cause." Peter H. Penwell was sixty-six years old. He was described as a "stump shouldered, white haired old man. He sold soap which he carried in a little tin box slung over his shoulder and was a quasi doctor pretending to cure the headache with a certain kind of snuff that he had and by touching the spot mostly affected." Although from Erin Center, he was often at the corner of Lake and Water Streets.

According to Sheriff Houper, Penwell had a "particular problem." He was insanely jealous about his wife. Some young men teased him by telling him that while he was in Elmira she was in Erin being "false to him." Penwell and his wife had been married for only four or five years. She was seven years his junior. The paper noted they had not lived "very cheerily together." Saturday morning they decided they could not go on like this and agreed to a suicide pact. They both swallowed arsenic, but not enough to kill them, just to make them sick.

At five o'clock Penwell walked into his wife's sick room and said, "Parmelia, your time has come," and he bludgeoned her with an ax and then took a razor to his own throat.

His wife yelled, "Oh Rosanna, Rosanna" calling for her sister in the next room who could not save Parmelia but saved Penwell.

When in a jail, the *Advertiser* reporter asked Penwell, "didn't you have any compunctions of conscience?'

The answer was "It did hurt my feelings a little, but she was willing to die and I thought I might as well end it here. I intended to cut my throat right afterwards. I didn't because the girl came in and stopped me."

The newspaper reported that on the day of his execution, "the crowd outside the jail was immense." It was kept from the execution ground by a detachment of the 110th Battalion. At the gallows Penwell "did not flinch a particle but calmly waited for his coming death... with tears visible in his eyes...he said 'I hope all the gentlemen here today will take warning by me."

After the execution the crowd outside was allowed to join the 250 witnesses to see the scaffold.

LITTLE EGYPT ARRESTED.

Ashea Waba, twenty-three years old, an Algerian dancer known as "Little Egypt" was arrested on a charge of disorderly conduct at the close of a matinee at the Empire theater in Brooklyn. The arrest was made by Roundsman Brennan of the Bedford avenue station, who had been watching the girl performing a dance known as the muscle dance. The roundsman considered the dance improper.

"Little Egypt" will be remembered in this city, where she appeared at the Globe theater.

Little Egypt's arrest in 1910. From the Elmira *Star-Gazette* dated Sept. 15, 1900 page 5.

Elmira's Law and Order League

By Diane Janowski

On January 28, 1899 it was announced in the *Star-Gazette* that Elmira would have a new movement for a "thorough effort to better the city reputation." It was "open to every person who believes in, and wants to live up to the Ten Commandments."

The "Law and Order League" participants were our local "prime movers" most of whom were also members of the "Elmira 400" the upstanding citizens of our community. This League came together with a "well-formed plan of attack which is going to sweep Elmira clean and is going to change the name Elmira now has for immorality."

"It has come to that state where Elmira has a reputation all over the state for vice, immorality, and being an open town where most anything goes and this has gone far enough. Men, women, and children are seen intoxicated on the streets, houses of questionable character are being conducted with open doors, saloons are open on Sundays...."

The Leaguers took it upon themselves to make complaints to the police against saloons, prostitutes, and other vices in and around Elmira. One of the first charges rendered was against the Globe theater for "immoral and indecent performances." "The previous evening's midnight performance [April 22, 1899] of the "Little Egypt" burlesque company was cited. The Wednesday Morning Club called it "a company of lewd women led by a notorious courtesan called Little Egypt. (Little Egypt did get arrested in 1900 in Brooklyn for the same performance.) Attorney Lynch maintained that if the Mayor revoked the Globe's theater's license, the manager would have a good

OBSCENE DANCE ISN'T REPEATED

Law and Order League Hears of an Indecent Performance Planned at Road House and Promoters Lose Nerve.

Elmira *Star-Gazette* headline, May 29, 1909 page 2

case against them for liable damages. In the same meeting before Mayor Edgar Denton, the League complained of a performance of "Cymbelline" at the Park Church with a young actress appearing in tights. Attorney Lynch cautioned the Leaguers that this was an amateur church performance using its own members in the cast. Several months later the League complained about a boxing match that was to be held at the Maple Avenue Athletic Club. Complaints were also filed against the sacred concerts at Eldridge Park on several Sundays in 1899.

By 1902, lawyers reported problems because of the zeal of the Law and Order League to prosecute everyone and everything in its vice clean-ups. The League prosecuted saloon owners who sold liquor on Sundays. Lawyer Danaher stated that "in every case of arrests in this county for Sunday selling of liquor the grand juries had failed to find an indictment and so prosecution was impossible, and presumed, the grand juries voiced the sentiment of the community." The police department was also perturbed at the League's persistent efforts to help officers do their jobs.

In 1909, "there had been rumors on [Elmira's] streets that there was to be an exhibition of "Salome" dancing at a road house just outside of town. Sixty Leaguers piled into vehicles and quickly went to the establishment. Sure enough, two dancers, without much in the way of costumes charging $30 for the dance, were there. After an assessment of the situation, the Leaguers put a stop to it.

Again in 1909, two secret investigators from the New York State Excise department were in town to investigate the Patterson House on the corner of East Market and Baldwin Streets, also known as "The Hippodrome" because there was always "something doing."

And again in 1909, a state League publication rated the three top locations where liquors were being consumed. First, New York City, second, Buffalo, and third, was Elmira.

Over the next six months Law and Order Leagues sprang up in local nearby towns. People were willing to donate money, and funds were used to prosecute saloons, gambling establishments, drunken people, and

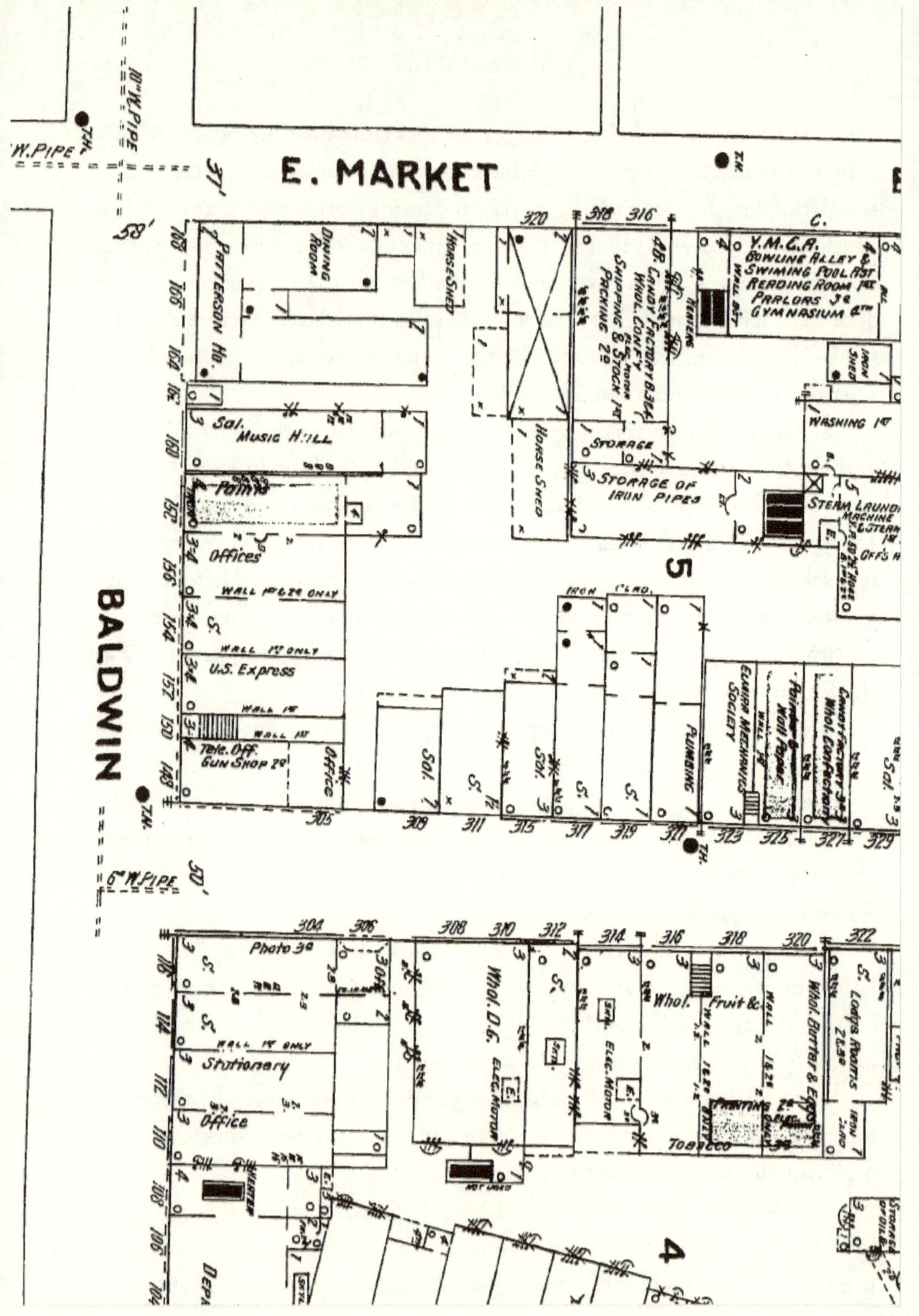

1903 Sanborn map showing the Patterson Hotel at the corner of East Market and Baldwin Streets.

disorderly houses. Names and addresses of people applying for liquor licenses were published. In 1909, Leaguers prosecuted two Railroad Avenue saloons for not opening their curtains on a Sunday. Open curtain laws on saloon windows allowed the public to see that nothing was happening inside.

In 1910, the Towanda, PA Law & Order League prosecuted several druggists for "dispensing cider of an unusually strong quality."

On a tip from the Law & Order League, on Saturday, September 4, 1915 Sherriff Biggs raided the Van Etten Soldiers and Sailors picnic and arrested a man running a "wheel of fortune." The sheriff "promptly put on the lid and called all bets off." In 1916 Leaguers also put a stop to bicycle vendors selling cigars and candy on the street.

The last mention that I found of the League in Elmira newspapers was 1924.

Sources:

Star-Gazette (Elmira, New York) 28 Jan 1899, Sat Page 8
Star-Gazette (Elmira, New York) 26 Apr 1899, Wed Page 7
Elmira *Gazette*. April 10, 1902
Star-Gazette (Elmira, New York) 29 May 1909, Sat Page 2
Star-Gazette (Elmira, New York) 05 May 1899, Fri Page 7
Star-Gazette (Elmira, New York) 10 Aug 1909, Tue Page 7
Star-Gazette (Elmira, New York) 07 Sep 1915, Tue Page 13
Star-Gazette (Elmira, New York) 26 Feb 1916, Sat Page 2

Postcard view of the First Baptist Church, publisher unknown. Courtesy of the Barnes Library.

First Baptist Church

By James Hare

When the first Methodist circuit rider arrived in the Chemung valley in 1792, he had been warned to be aware of "bears, blizzards and Baptists." Perhaps he was aware that "Baptist activity" in the area was underway. "Parson" Goff had been preaching to neighborhood gatherings in the vicinity of Wellsburg as early as 1789. Ironically, over two hundred years later in 2019, the United Baptists of Elmira and the New Beginnings United Methodists share the same building at 300 East Miller Street. Worshipping at separate times, they are friendly between services.

The Baptist congregation established in Wellsburg was not only the parent church for the Baptist community, but indeed the mother church for Chemung County. In 1829, the Southport and Elmira Baptist Church was organized. According to the Elmira *Telegram* on March 30, 1930, a council of churches "was constituted by delegates from the churches at Big Flats and Elmira and Springfield and Canton, Pennsylvania" to formalize the church a year after Elmira had been incorporated as a village. Two years afterward in 1831 the society was legally recognized by act of the Legislature and twenty years later on April 11, 1849, the act organizing the "Baptist Church and congregation of the Towns of Southport and Elmira was confirmed. On June 24, 1853, the name was changed to the First Baptist Church of Elmira."

The Reverend Philander D. Gillette, "an enthusiastic and eloquent" man is credited with the church's establishment and organization. Being married to a daughter of Jeffrey Wisner was an important connection. Charles Mathews Jr., wrote for the *Star-Gazette*, "for some time, meetings were held in private homes. In 1832, Jeffrey Wisner sold the present location of the church (121 West Church Street) to the body for $1.50 stipulating in the deed that unless a church building was erected there it should revert to his possession." The entire cost of the first structure was $954.

The first church was small, and by 1848, a larger building was needed. Dedicated on January 24, 1849, it seated "more persons than any other church in the village." (*Star-Gazette*, November 14, 2004) Thirty eight members had founded the church and during the first half of the 19th century the church thrived. In fact, the community of faith in Elmira, in all denominations, witnessed a growth in numbers and new construction as the second half the century got underway in what today would be considered downtown. The following churches were built: the Hedding Methodist Episcopal Church in 1852 (now the Neighborhood Community Center), cornerstone for St. Peter and Paul's laid in 1854, the current Trinity Episcopal Church held its first service in 1858, a new building for the First Presbyterian Church (where Elm Chevrolet now stands) in 1862, Lake Street Presbyterian Church in 1862, Grace Episcopal Church in 1866, St. Patrick's Church dedicated in 1872, the Park Church in 1875, the First Methodist Church rebuilt after fire in 1886, formerly on Baldwin Street, and the First United Church of Christ (the German Church) in 1899.

It should also be noted that beyond "downtown" St. Casimirs was dedicated in 1889 as was North Presbyterian Church. The following year St. John's at the corner of Lake and Second Streets was dedicated. All of this is a remarkable statement about religion in Elmira at that time.

Remarkable and long serving religious leaders also dominated the landscape. The Rev. Thomas K. Beecher was in charge of Park Church from 1854 until his death in 1900. The Rev. George McKnight was at Trinity Episcopal from 1869-1905.

Father James J. Bloomer was priest at St. Patrick's Church from 1870-1931, and the Rev. William T. Henry, D. D. was pastor at the First Baptist Church from 1877-1921, his first and only pastorate.

Like the Rev. Beecher and Father Bloomer, Dr. Henry was a builder. He was born January 16, 1849 in New York City. He graduated from Colgate Academy in 1870 and from Madison (now Colgate University) in 1874 at the head of his class at both schools. In 1876, he graduated from Hamilton Theological Seminary and his first call was Elmira in 1877. He never left.

When Dr. Henry first arrived the membership of the church was 346. At his 25th anniversary membership stood at 1,185. The second building had been built in 1848, raised and enlarged in 1875. Damaged by fire in

1880 it became necessary to build a new church. In 1889 it was demolished in preparation for new construction. The current building was designed by Pierce and Dockstader (forerunner of Pierce and Bickford). It is Romanesque in style and uses Hummelstown sandstone trim to ornament the windows and doors. Roger Reed in a book on Pierce and Bickford, wrote that it was, "imposing for its bold silhouette."

The Elmira *Daily Gazette and Free Press* reported on May 16, 1892, "Yesterday was the day set apart for the first service... It was a typical spring day, warm, fragrant and bright. The feelings of nature seemed to blend poetically with the inspirations of the 1,300 worshippers who thrice gathered within the walls of the new church and listened to the stirring and earnest words of prayer and praise and the beautiful music of the sweet toned organ accompanied by hundreds of voices."

The Rev. Beecher and many others shared the message with Dr. Henry.

On September 20, 2009 the First Baptist Church held a Decommissioning Service. In 2011, the building was sold to private interests.

Burger Chef ad,
Elmira *Star-Gazette*,
July 1, 1970 page 17.

Dean Martin's Gold Diggers,
Elmira *Star-Gazette*,
August 2, 1970 page 44

Summer 1970s Style

by Diane Janowski

Having been born in August I am naturally drawn to the summer months. Elmirans had plenty to do the summer of 1970. I was only ten so I was mostly limited to swimming at Brand Park pool, waiting for the Mr. Softee ice cream truck, and going to Eldridge Park.

"Midnight Cowboy" was playing at the Elmira Drive-In. Collette, an exotic dancer from New York City, was entertaining at the Polynesian Room at the corner of Main and Water Streets.

You could eat clams raw or steamed at Rosar's Grill on John Street in Horseheads. The Pour House on Grand Central Avenue was serving their Friday Night Sea Food Smorgasbord. Loblaw's grocery on William Street was selling watermelons for 69 cents with a coupon. Kool-Aid stands were asking 3 cents for a "whole glass." Burger Chef on Lake Road next to Nichol's had a special on hamburgers 59 cents buy one get one free. Salisbury steak dinners for $1.59 were the special at Roy Russell's restaurant on North Main Street on June 30. Kresge's on West Water Street had a sale on women's acetate underwear for 38¢ a pair. Downtown clothing merchants agreed that women's pantsuits were "the item of the season." Merchants held Frontier Days their summer sidewalk sales the week of July 26. U-pick sweet cherries were available at many local farms. Karam's Giant Market on Mt. Zoar Street was selling jumbo bunches of fresh dill for 29¢.

The Bootery on North Main Street had a half-off sale on "New Look Summer '70" shoes. Prices from $5 to $16.99. Rosenbaum's parrot Rosie had a "Bird-day Party" on July 9 at their West Water Street location with smashing bargains. Linberger's meat market on 14th Street offered "skinned and de-veined baby beef liver." Mr. Panosian's Junior Colony at South Main and Henry Streets had a 50% off all remaining summer clothes for boys and girls. Winnick's Army and Navy received a shipment of 1,000 pairs of bell bottom pants in solids, stripes, denims, plaids, rainbows, and cords.

Fashion trends were predicting the "poncho" to be a big look that year. The People's Place in Midtown Plaza advertised super selections of mod clothes including bell bottoms and sun glasses. Sportogs on North Main Street had a half-off sale on culottes, maxi coats, slacks, and pant suits. The Lovely Shop on College Avenue advertised a 2 for 1 dress sale.

Our area had hundreds of new young people in the summer workforce. Elmira Free Academy graduated 509 students, Southside graduated 420, and Horseheads graduated 479.

Elmira College's summer courses included 20th Century China, The American Urban Crisis, Understanding Art, Money and Banking, and 19th Century Russian Literature. Elmira Business Institute offered summer classes including Stenoscript, Card Punch Data Processing, and Introduction to Programming Language.

Our own Geoff Bodine was racing every Saturday at Shangri-La Speedway in Owego. The New York State Dune Buggy Championship was held on July 4, 1970 in nearby Erin. A & W Rootbeer was open for business in Elmira Heights (today's Big Top ice cream stand). Dean Martin's "Gold Diggers" appeared at the 128th Chemung County Fair. The Mall (today's Arnot Mall) had a big July 4th fireworks show with the stores staying open until midnight with "an explosion of values in every store."

In July many playgrounds held hula hoop and frisbee contests. On July 6 a crowd of 15,000 at Eldridge Park watched four parachutists freefall from 7,500 feet into Eldridge Lake.

On July 6, William Shatner opened in Corning Summer Theater's presentation of "The Tendertrap."

The worst day of my summer, and probably many others, was always the day that Brand Park pool closed for the season.

Merchants' Frontier Days,
Elmira *Star-Gazette*,
June 11, 1970

NYS Dune Buggy Championships,
Elmira *Star-Gazette*,
July 4, 1970, page 9

Frontispiece of 1887's "John Arnot, Jr., Late a Representative." Courtesy of Wikipedia.

John Arnot, Jr. , The First Mayor

By James Hare

"A gas explosion occurred in the vault of the Chemung Canal Bank on Water Street, at 9AM today, which made a loud report heard a block away, and for a time created the greatest excitement. John Arnot, congressman from this district and president of the bank, had been seriously injured. A crowd soon collected and it was necessary to station a police officer at the door to keep the many eager ones from crowding into the bank." According to biography file 02-250 at the Chemung County Historical Society, the newspaper of October 20,1884, went on to report that the vault had been newly built. It was the custom for the last person in the vault at night to turn off the gas. For some reason, either negligence or malfunction, gas had filled the vault overnight. When Arnot went into the vault that morning, lit the gas and unlocked one of the safes he came out and remarked, "that there was a smell of something in the vault like kerosene oil." As he started to enter the vault a second time, a terrific explosion blew him across the room and threw him, "violently" against the large office desk. His hands and face were badly burned and it was feared that he had been otherwise injured. Damage to the bank was extensive.

Mr. Arnot recovered, but died two years later. The paper noted in his obituary, "He was a man of large stature and admirable physique, who gave promise of living twenty years, previous to the unfortunate occurrence two years ago."

The bank (located at the current site of the Chemung County Historical Society) had been founded in 1833. At the time of his death, the Arnot family controlled the bank and John Jr. was the cashier. In effect he was "president" of the bank. He had been selected cashier in 1852, when his father (who had been cashier) became the president.

Upon the death of John Arnot Sr., the bank chose not to elect another president, thus the cashier, in effect ran the bank. On the letter head of the bank stationary a "black line opposite the word president" was displayed.

John Arnot Sr. came from Scotland, and settled in Elmira in 1819 as a merchant. In 1824, he married Harriet Tuttle. He partnered with her father erecting the first brick store in Elmira. Later he built a foundry on Lake St. and in 1842 became cashier at the Chemung Canal Bank. Eventually, in 1857 he would take over controlling interest of the bank. The Arnots would have six children: Stephen Tuttle Arnot, John Arnot Jr., Matthias Arnot, Marianna Arnot Ogden, Aurelia Arnot and Fanny Arnot Haven.

Service was the hallmark of John Arnot Jr. He was a life long Democrat. According to the Elmira *Telegram* on November 21, 1886, "His personal popularity was so great that he could at any time have any office he wished in the gift of the people of Elmira." He was three times president of the village of Elmira, 1859, 1860 and 1864. When Elmira became a city in 1864, Arnot was elected the first mayor and subsequently elected mayor in 1870 and 1874. In 1882 he was elected a member of Congress as a Democrat in a heavily Republican district and re-elected in 1884 as the nominee of both the Democratic and Republican parties. The *Weekly Advertiser* of October 21, 1884 noted that the nomination of Mr. Arnot, upon his record as a legislator…and coming, as it does, from a political party opposed to the party of his life long affiliation is an indication of progress in politics as hopeful as it is creditable to all concerned."

John Arnot Jr. had extensive business and social commitments and connections. He had pews in the Park Church and Trinity Episcopal Church. John Arnot Sr. had left an estate of $6,000,000 ($144,000,000 in 2016 dollars). His estate had included the Chemung Canal Bank, blocks of real estate in the city of Elmira, steamboat interests in Seneca Lake, the Elmira gas works and extensive coal producing properties in Pennsylvania and Ohio. John Jr. was sole owner of the brewery T. Briggs and Company on East Second Street.

The obituary in the *Telegram* of November 21, 1886 included the following tribute, "Elmira loses fifty good citizens by the death of John Arnot, said a well known lawyer...he was the richest, the most influential, the most popular and the most generous citizen of Elmira" and Colonel Archie Baxtor, who Arnot had defeated for Congress in 1882 said, "Although he defeated me for Congress, I would take off my shoes and stockings this moment and walk to Washington in my bare feet to restore him to his health."

The funeral was held at the residence on the corner of Park Place and Clinton Street, the current site of Arnot Park. The Rev. Thomas K. Beecher and the Rev. Dr. McKnight officiated. The grocers, hardware dealers and the dry goods businesses closed their stores from 2 o'clock to 4 o'clock the day of the funeral. Also closing were the city offices.

John Arnot Jr. was survived by his wife Elizabeth Hulett Arnot, a son, John H. Arnot who never married and a son Matthias C. Arnot, who was twice married with no children. His daughter, Harriet, married James B. Rathbone and had three children.

Eldridge Park's casino. Photo by Elisha VanAken, courtesy of the Barnes Library.

Elmira's Casino

by Diane Janowski

Eldridge Park's casino in the 1870s had no chips, cards, tables, or slot machines. It was an ice cream parlor with porches with 360° views on three floors, a walkway on the fourth, and an observation deck on the fifth floor. It cost $18,000 to build, and was painted yellow and white like the other early buildings in the park.

In June 1908, vaudeville actor Harry DeVonde was in town appearing at the Queen City Gardens theater on Westside Avenue. Harry just so happened to be a daredevil, and planned "the most sensational high wire act ever seen in this section of the country" – his "Slide for Life" many feet in the air across the whole lake. He convinced park manager E.M Little to let the Elmira Water, Light & Railroad Company to string a zip line wire from the top of the casino to a "large willow tree on the opposite side of the lake near the bear pit." He wanted to do four shows – two in the afternoons and two in the evenings. His evening shows had an "extra something special" – FIRE. He said he would be "enveloped in flames" for added excitement during the trip. Near the opposite shore he planned to "plunge into the water from his elevated position."

Harry was also Hollywood actor Chester DeVonde's brother. He sometimes billed himself as "Daredevil DeVonde" performing this feat in parks of many large cities on the East Coast.

During an early practice session for his event, the wire snapped and Harry fell onto the grass. The wire was re-hung under his personal supervision and on July 4, 1908, he did perform his daring act at Eldridge Park. "Spectators held their breaths as his figure traveled high in the air at a rapid rate of speed supported only by a wire which is invisible to the naked eye." The first show went OK but the evening's "envelope of flames" aspect of the act proved to be not such a good idea after all. Harry received severe burns on the first night that not even the cool lake water could soothe, putting an end to next day's performances.

The show must go on and four days later, Miss Elvina Richards of New York City, and also of the vaudeville players troupe performing at the Queen City Gardens, used the same zip line to perform her own "Slide for Life." Elvina was "suspended by her neck from a trolley wheel that traveled along the top of the wire. She wore a fancy costume with tights, and carried a lighted torch in each hand. There was a large crowd on the shores of the lake to witness the wonderful act and the performer was liberally applauded." Eldridge Park's management held over Elvina's act for several weeks.

By 1911, the casino had outlived its usefulness. It was more than forty years old and in decrepit condition, and the city decided to raze the building. In spring 1911, the casino was razed and the area was graded. Shrubbery and sidewalks were built "to be inviting and of use to the public." Some of the casino's lumber was used to build a music hall and another portion was used for "another large building."

With the money saved from the razing of the casino rather than its restoration, the city bought two elks that arrived at the park in time for its May 30, 1911 opening. Two new bears to replace two that had died, were ordered for the bear pit but according to the *Star-Gazette* article of May 3, 1911, "there was a scarcity of these animals this season, and the park commissioners will be forced to wait for a few weeks until they can be procured by the New York dealers."

Sources:

Star-Gazette (Elmira, New York) · Fri, Nov 17, 1911 · Page 7
Star-Gazette (Elmira, New York) · Mon, Jun 29, 1908 · Page 9
Star-Gazette(Elmira, New York) · Sat, May 20, 1911 · Page 7
Star-Gazette (Elmira, New York) · Thu, Jun 25, 1908 · Page 9
Star-Gazette (Elmira, New York) · Tue, Aug 18, 1908 · Page 3
Star-Gazette (Elmira, New York) · Wed, Apr 4, 1906 · Page 5
Star-Gazette (Elmira, New York) · Wed, Jul 8, 1908 · Page 10
Star-Gazette (Elmira, New York) · Sat, Jun 27, 1908 · Page 2
Star-Gazette (Elmira, New York) · Fri, Jun 26, 1908 · Page 4
Star-Gazette (Elmira, New York) · May 3, 1908 · Page 7

John Purroy Mitchel, James Watson Gerard and John Barry Stanchfield (in the fur collar) in 1917. Photo courtesy of Wikipedia.

John B. Stanchfield

By James Hare

Baseball lore has it that the curve ball was invented in the early 1870's, maybe as early as 1867 by Candy Cummings. There are, however, those who credit an Elmiran, John B. Stanchfield, with the honor.

According to his obituary on June 26, 1921 in the New York *Times*, in the year 1874, "A pitcher on the Amherst baseball team, Mr. Stanchfield, is credited with having thrown the first curved ball. An elderly, strong opinionated Professor of Physics devoted a portion of his lecture one day citing formulae to prove that a horizontal curve to a hurried sphere violated all laws of nature and physics.

'Your formulae may be correct professor' spoke up Stanchfield, 'but if you come out on the diamond this afternoon, I'll prove that I can throw a curve.' The professor was placed back of the catcher that afternoon behind the end of a brick wall. Near the other end of the wall, out of sight of the physicist and the catcher, pitcher Stanchfield threw what is known as a round-house curve into the catcher's glove.

The demonstration filled the professor with the ambition to revise his physics formulae."

J. Sloat Fassett, who described himself as an, "associate and rival and political opponent and yet always the warmest of personal friends ever since we were little boys" was quoted in the June 25, 1921 *Star-Gazette* saying, "I do not think I will be accused of exaggerating when I say that John B. Stanchfield, at his death, was easily the leading trial lawyer in the United States, and he was regarded as at the head of the Bar in the great city of New York."

Stanchfield had been prominent in politics as well as the law. Before the age of 25 he was first elected to two terms as Chemung County District Attorney from 1880-1885. Following that he served a term as Mayor of Elmira from 1886-1888 and then two terms in the New York State Assembly from 1895-1896. In 1900 he was the Democratic candidate for governor of

New York and a year later was nominated by his party for the office of United States Senator.

In addition to law and politics he was a close personal friend of Olivia and Sam Clemens (aka Mark Twain). Indeed he referred to himself as "Mark Twain's lawyer." According to Dr. Matthew Seybold of Elmira College, Editor of MarkTwainStudies.org, on September 19, 2018, Stanchfield's wife Clara was, "Livy Clemens' lifelong friend and fellow Elmira College alumna, after whom she named her second daughter." Indeed, the Clemens may have played matchmaker between Clara and John. Seybold notes that, "before Stanchfield married, John and Sam had frequented the same billiard parlors, both using aliases." Apparently, in addition to being "amiable" drinking buddies and billiard partners, Stanchfield and Clemens enjoyed card playing and gambling. In Mark Twain In Elmira it is reported that Clemens was playing euchre at the home of Henry H. Rogers (who ran Standard Oil and was a financial advisor and close friend of Clemens) in New York City and said, "a small stake was involved which he told us wasn't big enough to insure him his car fare home, 'But', said he, 'John Stanchfield is teaching me a brand new game and when I get proficient in it and have it mastered, I'm going to introduce it up there, and I'll have Rogers' clothes."

Stanchfield, as noted had an illustrious legal career. Admitted to the bar in 1878, he became a partner with David B. Hill, a former mayor and eventually governor of New York State. In 1885, when Hill became chief executive, Stanchfield became co-partners in the law firm Reynolds, Stanchfield and Collins a forerunner of the firm Sayles & Evans in today's Elmira. When the Chemung County Bar Association met to pay tribute at Stanchfield's death, President Boyd McDowell said, "Mr. Stanchfield proved his versatility as a lawyer in every phase of endeavor professionally... To name the occasions when his extraordinary abilities in this direction were displayed would be to catalogue the most famous cases of the last decade and a half."

In one of his cases, Forbes vs Taylor in 1894, Stanchfield established the right of non-discrimination based on the Fifth Amendment. The circumstances of the case were that some sophomores at Cornell University in attempting to break up a banquet of the freshmen class had prepared to release

STUDENT TAYLOR'S CASE.

The Grand Jury Will Do Nothing Now Pending the Court of Appeals Decision.

Ithaca, N. Y., May 17.—The special term of Supreme Court and Court of Oyer and Terminer, with grand jury, reconvened this morning to further investigate the chlorine case. Judge Forbes failed to arrive on the morning train, but sent an order to the clerk to open court, stating that he would be in Ithaca at 4 p. m. In consequence of the Judge's absence and the fact that Judge Andrews has granted a stay in Taylor's case, the grand jury will not do anything in the chlorine case until Judge Forbes arrives. It is probable that they will then adjourn until June or July to await the decision of the Court of Appeals.

Star-Gazette (Elmira, New York)17 May 1894, page 7

a quantity of chlorine gas. According to a description of the case from courtlistner.com it was a "form of that species of arrogance or outrage popularly known as hazing." During the evening, while the banquet was in progress the gas from two jugs in the kitchen below was released via tube threw a hole bored in the ceiling and floor above. The gas caused the death of a "colored servant" (sic) and affected a number of students. Stanchfield advised his client Taylor not to answer any incriminating questions at the Grand Jury hearing, resulting in Taylor being charged with contempt of court. Stanchfield's position was upheld upon appeal to the Supreme Court, thus establishing a defendant's right to "Plead the Fifth." (National Cyclopedia of American Biography). It meant that a witness was the one to decide what might and what might not incriminate, and not the judge before whom he was testifying.

John B. Stanchfield died at the age of 66 at his home in Islip, Long Island. He was born in Elmira in 1855, and graduated from Elmira Free Academy in 1872 going off to college and law school. He married Clara Spaulding in 1886 and had two children. In 1906, they relocated to New York City because of the necessities of his legal career. His death in 1921, came after a ten day battle with kidney disease. He and his wife are encrypted in the mausoleum in Woodlawn Cemetery.

Bears and Monkeys in Elmira

by Diane Janowski

A bear pit was completed at Eldridge Park the last week of June 1891. Two caverns and a pen were afforded for 3 bears. It cost nearly $3,000 and was fifty-feet long and twenty-feet wide lined with brick and stone.

On July 4, 1892 a group of fifty men surrounded the bear pit and fed the bear peanuts. One of them threw in a large firecracker and the bear "retreated into his own private quarters."

On August 18, 1895, a "Big Bear Fight" happened between the three bears in the pit. "Queen" the large Rocky mountain black bear had frequently fought with the young cinnamon bear (a gift of city attorney John McDowell.) Queen "gave the cinnamon bear a death blow." Park Superintendent Thomas Pardoe said the animals were horribly cut and torn. The zookeepers "drove the large bears into their dens with blows from a heavy iron pole."

In June 1896 the park had a pair of bear cubs. On June 16 one of the cubs had had enough of captivity and climbed out of the pit. His disappearance was noted by the frantic actions of the mama bear. Park employees chased the poor baby through the park, and finally returned him to his mother.

Opening day in 1902 noted that the bear pit was the hit of the park with no less than 50 spectators at the attraction at all times.

The first municipal golf course in the area was at Eldridge Park in 1923. It had six holes – all of them "short enough for iron shots." Because it wasn't much of a course, nobody showed interest and it was abandoned in 1925.

The *Star-Gazette* reported in 1936, six rhesus monkeys were purchased from Camden, New Jersey and arrived by express train on July 31. It was hoped that they would help bring more tourists to the park. In less than a week, Sammy, Chet, Ozzie, Kelly, Junie, and Toots proved to be the hit of Elmira entertaining the crowds from "dawn until long after dusk." "Sammy

New Monkey Family Proves Popular With Visitors to Eldridge Park

A CENTER of attraction at Eldridge Park are the six monkeys recently obtained by concessionaires. Perhaps a trifle apprehensive is the little fellow at the left, top, as he stares at the cameraman. At the right top, one of the entertainers is enjoying a mid-morning meal. A throng about the cage is shown below.

New monkey family photo in the *Star-Gazette* August 6, 1937

was the oldest, biggest, and ugliest of the performers. Oscar is next in size, Junie is long and thin, Kelly is chunky and small, Toots is Kelly's girlfriend, and Chet is the smallest and most popular." The monkeys preferred lettuce to peanuts, but bananas were of course their favorite food.

Earlier that summer the roller coaster opened creating "fresh interest." According to the *Star-Gazette* of the same day, "Long waiting lines [for the coaster] are the rule on busy nights." City Superintendent Fred Wright estimated that on several weekends that summer, crowds exceeded 7,500.

During the Works Progress Administration (WPA) years, improvements to the park provided jobs for 70 WPA workers lasting about six months. The 1939-40 project had an expenditure of $28,000, with the WPA paying $20,000 and the city paying $8,000. Mayor Maxwell Beers thought it was too much for the city's part. City Manager Colus Hunter was "not enthusiastic" about the project and on its first vote rejected it. The project included a concrete bridge and culvert over the lake's outlet (near today's Thunderbirds ride), demolition of the bear pit, and a new road around the north end of the lake. New benches and picnic tables were also added. The cement and brick refuse from the bear pit was used in the dike for Newtown Creek at Sullivan Street.

In 1941, the WPA resumed work at Eldridge with new fireplaces, picnic houses, and some more new roads.

Also, on September 18, 1941, a monkey escaped for the second time that summer from the monkey house. At some point the next day, it was seen swinging in the rafters at the Elmira Foundry. The next day he was spotted near the Reformatory. Two days later he was seen at the top of Hamilton Hall on Elmira College's campus. That Friday night he climbed into a dorm window and surprised a student doing homework. Saturday and Sunday brought a "monkey frenzy" to the college neighborhood. Hundreds of children chased him, "dogs barked," hundreds of cars of lookers jammed the campus area. The monkey snickered at the crowd from up in the trees. Patrolman Edwin Dyer said, "the congestion was worse than in Elmira's business section at the peak of the Christmas season." Neighbors made homemade traps. A net almost caught the poor fellow.

Rifle Ends Treetop Career Of Escaped Park Monkey After Trap Attempts Fail

Two .22 calibre rifle bullets this morning ended th
career of the playful monkey that escaped from its Eld
ridge Park cage last Wednesday morning and had enter
tained hundreds of Elmirans since.

The little animal was shot by Robert Long, Eldridg
Park concessionaire, while it was perched in a tree at th
northeast corner of Washington and College Aves., at abou
9 a. m. today.

Image from *Star-Gazette* (Elmira, New York) Sept 22, 1941 · Page 3

The crowd was too much for the police force to handle, and I am sorry to report that on September 22, 1941, after futile attempts to capture it, the monkey was shot and killed by Robert Long, a concessionaire of Eldridge Park, on the northeast corner of Washington and College Avenue.

Sources:

Star-Gazette (Elmira, New York) June 26, 1891 page 5
Star-Gazette (Elmira, New York) June 22, 1891 page 7
Star-Gazette (Elmira, New York) July 5, 1892 page 7
Star-Gazette (Elmira, New York) June 18, 1896 page 3
Star-Gazette (Elmira, New York) May 30, 1902 page 7
Star-Gazette (Elmira, New York) March 3, 1936 page 2
Star-Gazette (Elmira, New York)July 31, 1937 page 2
Star-Gazette (Elmira, New York) May 26, 1939 · Page 22
Star-Gazette (Elmira, New York) Nov 27, 1939 · Page 8
Star-Gazette (Elmira, New York) Apr 5, 1940 · Page 9
Star-Gazette (Elmira, New York) Sept 18, 1941 page 17
Star-Gazette (Elmira, New York) Sept 22 1941 page 3
Star-Gazette (Elmira, New York) Oct 15, 1941 page 11
Star-Gazette (Elmira, New York) June 17, 1947 page 14

A KEY CITIZEN — Ella Fitzgerald receives a plaque and the key to the city from Elmira Mayor John M. Kennedy at festivities in the Elmira Armory following Miss Fitzgerald's performance at the Samuel Clemens Center Saturday night. George P. Zurenda (left), president of the Chemung County Performing Arts Inc., looks on.

Image from *Star-Gazette* (Elmira, New York) · Sun, Oct 23, 1977 · Page 1

Opening Night

By James Hare

Upon receiving the key to the city from Elmira Mayor John M. Kennedy, Ella Fitzgerald said, "It isn't the size of the city that is important. It's the people, and I've received so much love in this city."

The *Sunday Telegram* of October 23, 1977 noted that, "...Miss Fitzgerald completed the ingredients Saturday night for the gala opening of the Clemens Center, an event that should keep people talking for weeks."

Before the show began the audience was "amazed." The theater had been repainted and refurbished with the interior capturing "a feeling of the past while promising a great future." When the organ and the organist, "rose slowly from the orchestra pit accompanied by their own thunderous sound, it was symbolic of a revitalized Elmira rising from the mud and ruin of 1972."

Twenty five years earlier, in September of 1952, another capacity crowd had jammed the "new" Elmira Theater for two opening night stage and screen performances celebrating, as Mayor Emory Strachen noted, "a new era for the entertainment field in the Elmira area." (*Star-Gazette* September 27, 1952). The program opened with the playing of the "Star Spangled Banner" and a color guard from the Harry B. Bentley Post American Legion. A 300 million candlepower search light had rotated around the sky for four hours to add a Hollywood touch. When it first became noticed, the newspaper received calls reporting "a flying saucer." Bob Hope sent a congratulatory message, "Tops, congratulations to you and a warm greeting for the reopening of the Elmira Theater. Understand you've spent a quarter of a million and that's important money, even to Crosby." The theater had been purchased by the One-Five-Three Corporation formed under the leadership of William J. D. Dipson of Batavia, John Osborne of Wheeling, W. Virginia with David Mandeville of Elmira.

The ancestry of the Clemens Center/Elmira Theater can be traced back to Monday, December 21, 1925 when an enthusiastic and admiring audience of 2,500 attended the official opening of the Keeney Theater. The

Star-Gazette headline two days prior read, "Half Million Dollar Playhouse Declared To Be Most Beautiful Between New York and Buffalo." The day after the opening the paper reported that, "from the opening playing of "America" by the Keeney orchestra of eleven skilled musicians while the huge audience stood to the last flicker of the "Ten Commandments" on the screen at 11 o'clock, it was a "continuous period of education, pleasure and high class entertainment." Lieutenant Governor Seymour Lowman, from Elmira, introduced Frank A. Keeney to cheers and applause. Keeney commented, "I like Elmira and it is gratification to know you like the theater. It is your theater—an Elmira product."

Coincidentally, on the very night of the opening, Sunday movies were legalized by an 8-4 vote of the City Council despite strong opposition by Elmira's Protestant churches, according to County Historian Tom Byrne. Democrats voted yes, the Republicans voted no.

Apparently this issue was so contentious that a year later a public referendum was being considered.

The idea of a new theater for Elmira was conceived a year prior to 1925. The Southern Tier Theater Company was formed in November of 1924 and property purchased by J. John Hassett was selected as the site. The president of the organization was Francis G. Maloney, who had been in charge of Rorick's Glen for years and Stafford D. Noble was the treasurer and oversaw the original stock issue which financed the construction of the theater. Construction began at the end of 1924.

At that point it was called the State Theater.

Frank A. Keeney was a prominent New York Theater owner, with playhouses in Brooklyn, New England and Williamsport. He took a twenty one year lease on the theater which was renamed The Keeney Theater.

Less than a year after the "grand opening" of the Keeney Theater under Keeney's management, on November 29, 1926 at 8:15pm the curtain rose for a gala performance celebrating the "Bernstein management of the new Keeney Theater." The *Star-Gazette* had reported on November 17, 1926 that the interests of Frank A. Keeney had been taken over by the William Bernstein estate. Benjamin and Harry Bernstein had been interested in the lease at the

New Keeney Theater, Photographed Friday, as Final Work Was Being Rushed

Photo taken on the Friday before the Monday opening. Star-Gazette (Elmira, New York) · Sat, Dec 19, 1925 · Page 11

time Keeney was selected. It had been decided to keep the name of the theater "Keeney's" and the policy was to have "the best vaudeville...and the best of pictures."

The Bernsteins were not present at the opening because of the death of the their grandmother that morning. Their attorney, Lewis Henry told the audience that, "the Bernsteins," who ran a chain of ten theaters, including four in Elmira "felt that strong competition had come to this city and it is no secret that they endeavored to obtain a lease of this building. Luck at first broke against them, and later broke for them and today they hold a lease of this handsome playhouse." The opening program of pictures and vaudeville won much praise.

The Flood of 1972 devastated downtown and specifically the Elmira Theater. In April of 1975 a citizens group was organized and began the process of buying and preserving the Elmira Theater as a performing arts center. George Zurenda, chairman of the Chemung County Performing Arts Inc. was quoted in the April 12, 1975 *Star-Gazette* said, "It's a bargain now, it would cost something like $5 million to build a similar facility, and we've got it right here." He went on to say that according to a study the acoustics of the theater "rank among the finest in the Eastern United States." The theater had been purchased by the Elmira Urban Renewal Agency with plans for demolition or sell it to the newly created Performing Arts group.

The theater would be renamed the Clemens Center.

LOOKING TO THE FUTURE—Arnold Breman, executive director of the Clemens center (left), and George P. Zurenda, who headed efforts to develop the center, stand on the steps being constructed for the new entrance to the old Elmira Theater. The center is expected to open in September.

Star-Gazette (Elmira, New York) · Thu, May 12, 1977 · Page 23

Taylor's Early Idea of an Airplane

A machine designed to fly, built by Mansel Taylor of this city more than 30 years ago, is shown above. Parts of this early plane will be carried up by Daniel J. Hungerford over the city at the Elmira Airport dedication today and Sunday. The remains of the plane were found several years ago on the Chemung River bank.

A photo of Taylor's ornithopter in the *Star-Gazette* dated September 10, 1927, page 4.

Fly Like a Bird

by Diane Janowski

Mansel Taylor had an idea in 1890 – an ornithopter or flapping-wing aircraft. Its appeal was that it would fly like a bird. He organized the Aerial Navigation Company of Elmira complete with a board of trustees.

Taylor was born on June 3, 1833 in Chester County, Pennsylvania. He came to Elmira sometime after 1850, but before 1876. The 1876 Elmira city directory lists him as selling fruit and oysters at 124 West Water Street.

According to the Elmira *Daily Gazette* dated September 14, 1897, he had a feed and seed store down stairs at 442 East Water, but on the second floor in his shop "is a machine, which if it fulfills the plans of its inventor will make a fortune for himself... and make the inventor's name a household word all over the world, and make Elmira a center of a great industry." Mr. Taylor kept his model carefully guarded in a room, and only he had a key. That newspaper also noted that a patent had been applied for and the papers all made out. Mr. Taylor refused to show the machine, or talk about its structure for fear of infringements. "Mr. Taylor has been working on the machine for fifteen years and thinks he has at last perfected it. He has studied aerial navigation all his life. He is about 65 years of age and has white hair. He is confident of the result and anticipates a fortune for all concerned. It will be the biggest thing that ever happened for Elmira if we located that factory here, and means wealth for all."

The same *Daily Gazette* reported, "The working model is about 3 feet square. At the bottom is a car for passengers which is hung on an incline. The motive power is to be furnished by huge wings, which work by means of levers, which are in turn operated by motors in the frame work above the car, but are controlled by means of apparatus attached to the car. From what can be learned, there are five huge wings which are to propel the flying machine. Four wings work together and the larger fifth wing alternates with the others. At the rear of the top is said to be a form of a fin which is operated from below, and steers like a huge bird. Whether or not the description is correct depends upon whether or not the meagre details learned for those who profess to know are correct.... The Queen City [Elmira] might have the honor of being the home of the first successful flying machine. The working model is built and has been tested. It is, of course, fragile and crudely built but what has been leaked out the test was a success beyond all anticipation and the owner is confident... to have at last solved the 'problem of the century.' The model and Mr. Taylor were [supposedly] at the Chicago World's Fair in 1893 and attracted much attention."

I did not find him listed as an exhibitor at the Chicago World's Fair of 1893.

I tried to find Mr. Taylor's patent in the US Patents Office, and found many for ornithopters, but not his, nor did I find one with five wings. Not to say it does not exist, but a quick search did not find it.

On February 4, 1910, the *Star-Gazette* reported that Mansel Taylor did go on to invent "Taylor's horseradish" which may be found in almost every home in the city. About his airship it said, "The inventor frankly admits that his airship was a failure, but it is not necessary for him to make any such admission regarding his bottled goods."

A week later in 1910, the *Star-Gazette* learned that Mr. Taylor was at it again. The February 16 edition claimed, "He is keeping his work secret and having various parts made at different shops. A new patent has been applied for. He expects to assemble the machine in the spring and test it in May. The July 6 edition said, "Experiments were being conducted with a new and improved "flying machine that will surpass the performances of any yet made."

I did not find that patent either. Unfortunately, Mr. Taylor died two years later in 1912.

Sometime around 1925, Daniel Hungerford of Elmira's "Rocket Car" fame, says that a fisherman found the shattered wreck of Mansel Taylor's plane on the banks of the Chemung River. It had been stored in a barn on East Hill, until apparently someone disposed of it in the river. Hungerford reclaimed the several aluminum wing parts, and promised that Taylor's invention "would fly" over the skies of Elmira. On September 11, 1927 during the dedication ceremony of the new Elmira airport on Caton Avenue in Southport, a Taylor wing piece was flown over the city in an airplane.

According to his Mansel's son, Harry Taylor, in 1927, "He [Mansel Taylor] did succeed in making a craft that would rise from the ground but could not make it fly any great distance and consequently the aerial company went out of existence."

The last advertisements I found for Taylor horseradish in many stores in central New York were dated 1961.

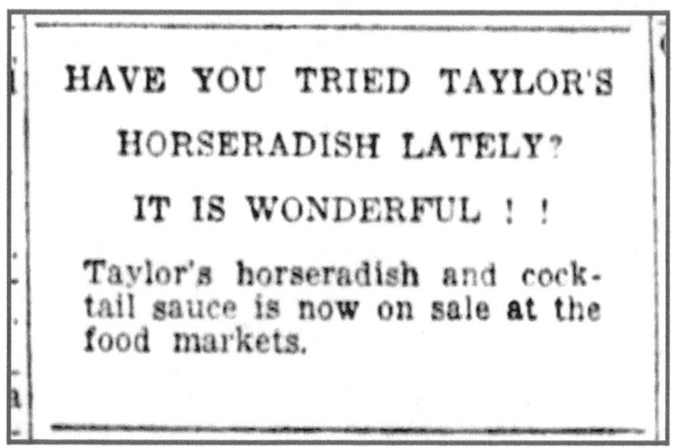

An advertisement in the Elmira *Advertiser* dated March 7, 1961, page 11.

Sources:

Star-Gazette (Elmira, New York) 10 Sep 1927, Sat Page 4
Star-Gazette (Elmira, New York) 14 Sep 1897, Tue Page 7
Star-Gazette (Elmira, New York) 04 Feb 1910, Fri Page 7
Star-Gazette (Elmira, New York) 16 Feb 1910, Fri Page 11
Star-Gazette (Elmira, New York) 17 Oct 1912, Thu Page 11
Star-Gazette (Elmira, New York) 12 Sept 1927, Thu Page 17

Raised to High Church Rank

The Rt. Rev. Monsignor James J. Bloomer

Star-Gazette (Elmira, New York) · Mon, Dec 22, 1930 · Page 17

Right Reverend Monsignor James J. Bloomer

By James Hare

"The sun of a beautiful January day streamed through the stained glass windows and seemed to focus rays of all colors of the spectrum on the scene in the sanctuary... The church, with normal seating capacity of 1,000 persons, was crowded three times beyond that. About 2,000 people were outside the church unable to enter...," reported the *Star-Gazette* on January 12, 1931. The scene was St. Patrick's Church. Faithful Catholics had gathered for the investiture ceremonies for Father James. J. Bloomer to be elevated to the papal rank of Domestic Prelate with the title Monsignor in the Household of Pope Pius XI.

On October 2, 1931, Bishop Francis O'Hern, head of the Rochester Diocese of the Roman Catholic Church saluted Monsignor Bloomer on his 90th birthday as the "Nestor of the clergy of the United States... I know of no other clergyman or prelate who has arrived at Msgr. Bloomer's age and is still active in the administration of a parish as large as St. Patrick's."

A little over a month later, on November 10, 1931, the *Star-Gazette* reported the death of Msgr. Bloomer, "The city of Elmira, the world of churchmen, the country—all have lost a great friend, a distinguished clergyman, a beloved priest, a servant of the people...." Monsignor Bloomer had been a priest for sixty three years, spending sixty one of them serving St. Patrick's Church.

James J. Bloomer was born in County Tyrone, Ireland, October 2, 1841. Four years later, his parents immigrated to the United States, settling in Philadelphia. He was raised in that city with a growing desire to become a priest. At age twenty-one, he qualified for entrance at St. Bonaventure College. At the Eastertide in 1867, he was to be ordained by the Rt. Rev. John Timon, Bishop of Buffalo. At that time the Southern Tier was part of the Buffalo Diocese. Unfortunately on the Monday of Holy Week preceding Easter and his ordination, the bishop died. It would not be until December 19,

1868 that the newly appointed bishop was able to ordain Father Bloomer. After a short stay in Buffalo, he was assigned to Salamanca, New York.

In 1870, the Catholics of Elmira lost two priests who had served them at St. Peter and Paul's Church. One of them, The Rev. Patrick Hopkins had been sent to Elmira to establish a new parish in the northwestern part of the city. On December 30,1869, he had purchased a site at the junction of Park Place and Main Street, the present location of St. Patrick's Church for $4,000 intending to build a church. His passing led to Father Bloomer's being called to carry on his work. Shortly after his arrival, the Rev. Peter Bede of St. Peter and Paul's died. Father Bloomer undertook administration of that church while continuing the work of building St. Patrick's until a replacement was found.

The history of the Roman Catholic faith in Newtown/Elmira dates back to an occasional visit of a missionary priest around 1800. Except for those visits, the only means which early settlers had of preserving their religious spirits were devotions practiced in their homes. As their numbers increased, about 1825, the First Presbyterian Church allowed their Catholic neighbors to use their wooden chapel at Church and Baldwin Streets. Eventually, on October 11, 1845, the first property purchased by a Catholic Church was acquired on the corner of East Market and High Streets, with the goal of building a church. On September 8, 1854, the cornerstone for the present day St. Peter and Paul's building was laid.

The ethnic diversity and geographic distribution of Catholics in the city, along with a likely increase in their numbers, were recognized during this period with the creation of three new parishes. A German-speaking parish of St. John the Baptist was formed around 1866-68, St. Patrick's parish in 1869 and St. Mary's in 1872 acknowledged the growth in the northwestern and southern portions of the city respectively.

Father Bloomer arrived in Elmira just as the new St. Patrick's parish was being formed to serve the growing Catholic flock. On July 4, 1870, before his arrival, the people of the new St. Patrick's parish held a big picnic and raised enough money, $1,600, to pay for a modest frame structure, to serve as their first church. Round about that temporary building, the outer walls of what is today the present St. Patrick's Church would be constructed.

Upon the laying of the cornerstone for the new building, the Elmira *Daily Advertiser* of July 1, 1872 reported that "the new church is on one of the most prominent and sightly spots in the whole city... St. Patrick's is to be one of the most imposing structures in our city...much credit is due to Rev. J. J. Bloomer, the pastor of the church, for his persistent energy and drive in hastening along the parish that has been under his charge to the work of building such an edifice for their worship." The estimated cost was $60,000. A little over two years later on December 14, 1874, the *Advertiser* noted that, "the new and beautiful St. Patrick's Church...was dedicated yesterday...in the presence of a very large congregation."

In January, 1883, Bishop Ryan of the Diocese of Buffalo (Elmira would not become part of the Diocese of Rochester until 1896) purchased property at the southwest corner of Park Place and West Clinton Street, diagonally opposite the church for $9,000. The site was to be used for the parochial residence which was to be built at an estimated cost of $6,500. The rectory would be the home of Father Bloomer, his elderly mother and a meeting place for parish groups such as the Ladies Aid Society. But there might have been more to this purchase than met the eye. In May, 1892, it was reported that a rumor had been revived that Father Bloomer anticipated turning the parochial residence into a school. The present building would be considerably enlarged. With plans prepared by the architectural firm of Pierce and Bickford, contractor Thurston and Haskell began construction of the school in late 1892. The project would cost approximately $35,000.

The school opened in 1894. The teachers were from the Sisters of Mercy from Batavia, New York. In June 1895, the first graduation took place. There were seven students, all girls. According to the *Courier Journal* of June 23, 1971, "The art and science of fund raising had not been developed when Msgr. James J. Bloomer faced his first deficit. He took the direct approach: levied a tax and dispatched collectors... With a new school to pay for out of Sunday income, Msgr. Bloomer needed an additional source of revenue for teacher's salaries. He taxed each wage earner 25-cents a month to get the money. The amount needed was little indeed by today's standards, $1,000 to pay five teachers."

Ausburn Towner in his *History of Chemung County*, when describing the building of St. Patrick's Church sums up the Rt. Rev. Msgr. James J. Bloomer best, "It's upbuilding is due to the zeal and intelligence of its pastor, the Rev. J. J. Bloomer, who to a Christian character added a business tact and judgment that eminently fit him for the position he occupies. He is a Philadelphian by birth and has won his own way in the world since a lad. He is much loved by his people and has the confidence and respect of the whole community."

Elmira's Urban Legend of Jimmy Doolittle

by Diane Janowski

There is a local legend about Jimmy Doolittle flying under the Lake Street bridge. Even when I was a little kid I remember people talking about it. I remember former Chemung County historian Archie Kieffer talking about it. Did it really happen? How should I go about finding if it is true?

First, I had to find out who was Jimmy Doolittle. Wikipedia says Doolittle was an American aviation pioneer. Born 1896 and died 1993. He received a medal of honor for his duty in World War II. During the 1920s he was a stunt pilot, so this was a good sign for me that it might have happened.

I learned that in October 1917 Jimmy enlisted in the US Signal Corps Reserve as a flying cadet. After World War 1, he pioneered many missions involving early navigational instruments in cross-county flights. He entered Massachusetts Institute of Technology with a master's thesis on aircraft acceleration tests. He received a doctorate in aeronautical engineering in 1925. Wikipedia says in 1929, he became "the first pilot to take off, fly and land an airplane using instruments alone, without a view outside the cockpit."

So, then I did some research to find out if Jimmy Doolittle was ever in Elmira by going through old newspapers of the time.

The answer was yes. The first mention of Jimmy in the *Star-Gazette* was September 3, 1927 when he was a guest at the opening of the Elmira Airport on Caton Avenue. He was called a "stunt ace" in that article.

On September 9, 1927 the *Star-Gazette* reported, "Famous Flyers Will Thrill Crowds Saturday and Sunday as Elmira's New Airport is Formally Opened." I knew I was getting closer. Maybe this would be the bridge story for which I was looking. An "air carnival" and gala occasion would mark the "epochal event in the city's history." Jimmy was scheduled for "exhibition flights" on both Saturday the 10th and Sunday the 11th.

It was a wonderful sight to see the ships line up at Elmira Airport. Here are ten vately owned 'planes in readiness for stunt or passenger flights. People thronged around the craft throughout Saturday and Sunday.

Airplanes lined up at the Elmira Airport on Caton Avenue on September 12, 1927. *Star-Gazette*, page 16

The newspaper said he "thrilled Elmirans for two days with his hair-raising stunts over the city. But, no mention of a bridge. The next day's evening *Star-Gazette* again said nothing about the bridge. The Monday *Star-Gazette* had a whole page of photos, but still not a bridge. So, I kept trying. Maybe he came back to Elmira at a later date.

I thought I had gotten lucky when I found that Jimmy came back to Elmira in 1930 for a State Airport meeting. Maybe this was it. More investigation proved nothing in the way of a bridge. So, finally I get to 1945 with still no answer, and decide I must have missed something somewhere.

Then I find a July 29, 1957 *Star-Gazette* editorial mention, "It doesn't seem many years ago that Jimmy Doolittle's stunting, including a sweep under the middle arch of the Main Street bridge, announced the dedication of an airport on Caton Avenue." The problem being that there was no author or reference to who said it. Ok, the legend was the 1927 visit after all, and it was the Main Street bridge - not Lake Street like I thought. Hmm, I need to go back and try again.

So I go back to the *Star-Gazette* dated September 12, 1927 page 17 where it reads, "...[Doolittle] piloted his Curtiss pursuit plane Vulture AC

2765 over the rooftops of downtown Elmira... In three exhibitions, two Saturday and one Sunday, he looped, side-slipped, spun, dipped, flew upside-down, and on a wing end, did a part of an outside loop for which he is famous and held the spectators rooted in their tracks by his dare-devil antics hundreds of feet above the earth." But again, no mention of a bridge. Why not? This should have been a huge story, but nothing. No story in the local newspapers, nor in state or national papers.

I spoke with archivist Rachel Dworkin at the Chemung County Historical Society. I hoped that because it was 1927 someone with a camera might have been there to snap the shot. I asked if they had any photos of Jimmy Doolittle's stunt at Main Street bridge. She said no.

Doolittle is mentioned in former Chemung County Historian Tom Byrne's History of Chemung County 1890-1975 as flying under the bridge, but no photos. At an event with 30,000 spectators in attendance how can there be no photos of the stunt?

Here's Lieutenant "Jimmie" Doolittle in his Curtiss pursuit 'plane, "Vulture," which he made do everything but talk. At that he made it "roar."

Jimmy Doolittle in his "Vulture" on September 12, 1927. *Star-Gazette*, page 16.

The last mention I found of Jimmy Doolittle in the *Star-Gazette* was dated January 20, 1992 in a column by Tom Page in which he was also trying to find out if the stunt actually occurred. A local man claimed he saw a video of the stunt at the Smithsonian's Air and Space Museum in Washington, DC. I contacted the museum last week and they have no such footage.

In one last attempt to prove or disprove the legend, I found Doolittle's "I Could Never Be So Lucky Again, An Autobiography" by James Doolittle and Carroll V. Glines. Jimmy did not mention Elmira in 1927 or the stunt in question, but did mention that he participated in "air races around the country" that year.

When, or if I find a photo of the Elmira bridge stunt I will share it with you.

Sources

Wikipedia
Star-Gazette (Elmira, New York) 09 Sep 1927, Fri Page 15
Star-Gazette (Elmira, New York) 05 Mar 1930, Wed Page 8
Star-Gazette (Elmira, New York) 29 Jul 1957, Mon Page 6

"Jimmie" Doolittle stunting, flying upside-down over airport.

Right on a wing-end, "Jimmie" Doolittle sailed along for a mile.

Jimmy Doolittle in his "Vulture" on September 12, 1927. *Star-Gazette,* page 16.

'Town Meeting' Broadcast Thursday Night to Detail War Memorial Drive Plans

A "Town Meeting of the Air" Thursday night at 7:30 over WENY will tell Chemung Countians more details of next Sunday's every-home canvass for War Memorial funds.

Star-Gazette (Elmira, New York) · Wed, Dec 12, 1945 · Page 8

War Memorial

by James Hare

"If Chemung Countians subscribe $750,000, the community center can be built as planned and can have a convertible arena floor that would permit a dance one night, ice hockey the next, basketball the next, a Scout Jamboree the next, a convention the next, a community-wide religious services on Sunday nights…."

"It is something Elmira needs and has needed", said Mrs. David Davies of 818 Broadway. Edwin Towner of 722 Dickinson Street commented, "I saw the plans in the paper and it's a good idea." "It will be some place for the young people to go. They really need something like it around Elmira. My husband, a serviceman, is for it." Stated Mrs. Dewey Cold of 261 Robert Street. (*Star-Gazette,* November 18, 1945 and December 6, 1945).

Thus, the concept, and the reaction to the proposal for a "block-long" civic center in downtown Elmira made in the fall of 1945. Indeed, what was being proposed was a "living" war memorial to honor those who had served in World War II. Former County Historian Tom Byrne noted in the March 1958 Chemung County Historical Society's *Journal* that, "there was bravery at the front, sacrifice at home. Two hundred and ninety-six of the 10,000 who served never returned alive. More than 600 were wounded. Another 100 were prisoners for varying periods. The contribution of the home front was war production—more than a quarter of a billion dollars worth of ordinance and vehicles from our county."

The War Memorial Committee was created by the Elmira City Council to, "investigate the feasibility of a memorial, suggest a title, location, means of raising funds and methods of maintaining the memorial. In September of 1945, the committee decided on a community center plan named the Elmira and Chemung County War Memorial.

In November of 1945, architect Robert T. Bickford proposed a "simple yet inspiring building," with a 5,000 capacity auditorium, convention rooms, community activity center and a Memorial Hall. According to Attorney Halsey Sayles, "several sites" were under consideration. "If sufficient funds are raised it is hoped to locate the War Memorial building on North Main Street or Park Place somewhere between Church and Fifth Streets.

A Memorial Corporation was created to receive funds, purchase a suitable site and plan for actual construction. Mr. and Mrs. William D. Schwenke of 602 Foster Avenue, were named to head the fundraising campaign. Blanche Schwenke had served as head of civilian mobilization and her husband was a veteran of World War I and had served as treasurer of the Harry B. Bentley American Legion Post.

A house to house canvass across the county was planned to raise the funds over a five week period from Thanksgiving to the end of December 1945. Air raid wardens, auxiliary firemen and auxiliary policemen were asked to help in the canvass because they were "good neighbors." "Give a bond you bought while the boys fought," was adopted as the slogan. The thought was a bond bought in the "boom days" of the war could be transferred to the project to "repay a debt the home front owes the military."

Meanwhile a proposal surfaced to build a Center similar to the Mayo Civic Auditorium in Rochester, Minnesota. Built in 1938, for under $500,000, that auditorium had been cited by the American Commission for Living War Memorials as an ideal center for a community the size of Chemung County. James O'Connor, president of the board which administered the Mayo building cautioned Elmirans against thinking their project could be operated on a "profit basis."

He wrote, "If a city attempts to make an auditorium self supporting, it will close the door on enterprises for the good of the man in the street."

Perhaps some foreshadowing events began to emerge. The door to door canvass scheduled for Sunday, December 16, 1945 was marred by near-zero temperatures resulting in less than half of the solicitors made their calls. Also, a proposal to combine the construction of a new million dollar county office building with the War Memorial project on the Lake-Williams-Market Streets. The site never got off the ground.

ARCHITECT'S SKETCH:

War Memorial Community Center

'Give a Bond You Bought While the Boys Fought'

BASED ON THE HOPES and aims of the War Memorial Committee, here is an architect's suggestion for the form of the War Memorial Community Center. Robert T. Bickford, architect, has submitted the elevation, above, and floor plans to the committee. Floor plans appear in today's Star-Gazette on Page 21.

Star-Gazette (Elmira, New York, Nov 29, 1945 page 19

By July 1946, it was clear that here would not be a War Memorial Civic Center in Elmira. While initially it appeared to have strong public support, by July only 4,800 of 16,000 potential contributors had donated to the project. On May 28, what was then rated as the "worst flood in history," swept the Chemung Valley sending the Chemung River to 20.7 feet above normal with a flood stage at 17-feet. Clean-up meant no municipal funds for the War Memorial. Finally, St. Joseph's Hospital undertook a fund drive to replace flood loses and the Harry B. Bentley Post started a campaign to build a recreation hall. Three fund drives at once was two too many.

The War Memorial fund stood at $177,000 in cash and pledges.

On Tuesday, July 30,1946 the Elmira and Chemung County War Memorial Inc. was dissolved. All funds collected, to the best of the ability of the committee, were to be refunded.

Rose Room

(Hotel Langwell)

Special Dinner
Christmas Day

12:30 to 2:30 p. m.
6 to 8 p. m.

Please make Reservations

Hotel Langwell's Rose Room dinner advertisement from the *Star-Gazette* Dec. 24, 1918 page 3.

An Elmira Christmas - 1918 Style

By Diane Janowski

100 years ago the first World War was recently over. The Spanish influenza epidemic was prevalent in the world and in Elmira. Soldiers were returning home to the US. How did we celebrate that wonderful holiday season?

Lots of folks "came home" to Elmira for their holidays. Austin Hassett, and Cornelius Donahue came from Holy Cross College in Massachusetts to be with their families. Chester Howell came home to his folks on Horner Street. His sister Edith had been sick with influenza for many days and was getting better. Miss Fanny Townsend of Cornell University spent the week with her parents on William Street.

The first Elmira soldier to return was Private Lawrence Personius. He came over on the "Leviathon." His return was a special present to his parents at 600 Sullivan Street. He was seriously wounded in the war, and arrived minus his left leg below the knee. Even in his rough condition, his mother was very happy to have him at home. He landed in the US unbeknownst to his family and friends. According to the *Star-Gazette* on December 21, 1918 he had been wounded on June 24, "shortly after the 108th was brigaded with the Fourth British Army and took up its position in Belgium. He was struck by a fragment of a bursting shell on the Flanders Front." His wound was so serious that gangrene set in. He expected another operation in New York City.

On December 23, 1918 a *Star-Gazette* headline said, "Elmira Schools with close for Christmas." Schools closed after classes the next day and would reopen the following Monday – five days later. The vacation was short due to "students had lost considerable time during the influenza epidemic."

Also, in the same newspaper, a holiday calamity had been averted by the Elmira police department who found a large bag containing three dresses, an eight-pound chicken, a quantity of sausage, a fountain pen, a wrist watch, and a number of Christmas presents belonging to Mrs. Wade Judge of 360 West Church Street. She had accidentally left the bag on the running board of her automobile when she drove off.

On Christmas Day 1918, Elmira's Arctic League dispensed gifts to 1,075 children in 391 households with the help of 40 automobiles and donations of $1,873.73.

Also, on December 25, the *Star-Gazette* reported that the "prettiest ball of the Christmas season was that given by Miss Jennie M. Curtis in the Federation Hall. The Jimmy Day Orchestra played and the group gave "encore after encore." The orchestra platform had been decorated with Christmas greens with a fancy Christmas tree. The reception rooms were transformed into a "bower of beauty." Red bells were suspended from the electric lights. Red candles were used on the larger tables and each had a basket of Christmas greens and poinsettias. Refreshments were served at midnight. Jenny's ball was very well attended and everyone had a delightful time.

On December 26 the *Star-Gazette* reported that the Salvation Army on Baldwin Street fed 1,600 guests on Christmas Day. Guests were served chicken, mashed potatoes, beans, pudding, and pie. Donations came from kettles "which adorned the streets for the past few weeks. They also sent 250 baskets with holiday fixings each feeding six people throughout our community.

On January 1, a "Big Special Holiday Matinee" at the Majestic Theater was held for the crowds. A Paramount film called "The Way of a Maid with a Man" and a superb big "girlie-girlie" musical comedy called "The Wandering Tourist" provided an ideal festive program. The Regent Theater also had a big show planned called "The Hun Within." The tag line said "Do not miss seeing the United States Secret Service catch the Hun-snakes."

Sources:

Star-Gazette (Elmira, New York) 31 Dec 1918 page 11

Star-Gazette (Elmira, New York) 31 Dec 1918 page 5

Star-Gazette (Elmira, New York) 26 Dec 1918 page 7

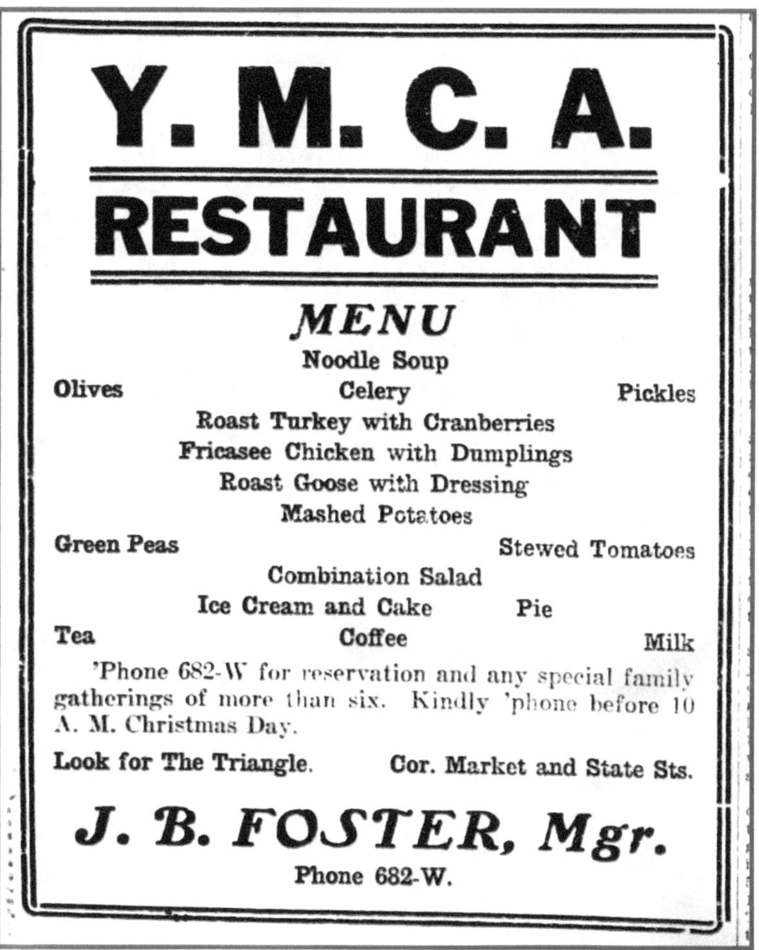

Y. M. C. A.

RESTAURANT

MENU

Noodle Soup

Olives Celery Pickles

Roast Turkey with Cranberries

Fricasee Chicken with Dumplings

Roast Goose with Dressing

Mashed Potatoes

Green Peas Stewed Tomatoes

Combination Salad

Ice Cream and Cake Pie

Tea Coffee Milk

'Phone 682-W for reservation and any special family gatherings of more than six. Kindly 'phone before 10 A. M. Christmas Day.

Look for The Triangle. Cor. Market and State Sts.

J. B. FOSTER, Mgr.

Phone 682-W.

YMCA's restaurant menu advertisement from the *Star-Gazette* Dec. 23, 1918 page 14.

Photographs of stairs at Woodlawn Cemetery. Photo by Diane Janowski.

Woodlawn Cemetery, Part One

By James Hare

A cemetery is a history of people, a perpetual record of yesterday and a sanctuary of peace and quiet today. According to Keith Eggener, Distinguished Professor of Architectural History, University of Oregon, in his 2010 book *Cemeteries,* there are 150,000 separate burial grounds in the United States covering two million acres. They range from churchyards, memorial parks, military cemeteries to "communities of exclusion" such as Boot Hill.

The development of Elmira's Woodlawn Cemetery was the result of a need for more burial space and an outgrowth of the "rural cemetery movement," which became increasingly more popular after 1830. In the June, 1983 Chemung County Historical Society's *Journal,* Janet Heller Howell wrote, "Woodlawn is a public treasure. Within this 184 acres and 15 miles of road are more than 800 trees, an outdoor sculpture garden of incredible beauty, and the vital history of all those who built the city. It is a commentary on our social history."

Elmira's earliest known burial ground was located on the land on the northeast corner of Sullivan and Water Streets. The July 5, 1925 *Telegram* reported that the bodies were never removed from the plot. In 1802, Jeffrey Wisner gave a tract of land just west of what is today, the former First Baptist Church (the eastern part of Wisner Park) for a burying ground. It is believed according to the September 8, 1961 *Star-Gazette* to have been the site of a former "Indian (sic) village of 40 wigwams." Wisner intended the cemetery to be used as a burying ground for the Village of Newtown.

In 1838, the Second Street Cemetery was opened. For twenty years thereafter all of Elmira's burials were made there. By 1858, it too had been filled. Ausburn Towner stated in his *History of Chemung County,* "many moved there and none moved away." In 1858, Samuel B. Strang, Ariel S. Thurston and Nathan Baker began to urge the necessity for a new cemetery according to

Towner. The state legislature authorized a loan of $10,000 for the purchase and by a margin of 22 votes the tax-payers agreed to a tax to pay it off. Francis Hall, who was President of the Village Board of Trustees, John Nicks, Nathan Baker and John Hill formed the committee which would select and purchase the site.

Janet Heller Howell described the process undertaken. The committee looked at "the Edmund Miller farm in Southport surrounding a natural pond, George W. Hoffman's farm, a broken rolling piece of ground with a pond and living springs of water; Simeon Benjamin's Pick-a-way Ground, fifth ward Southside; Mrs. Arnot's land on East Hill which was quickly ruled ineligible because of rocky ledges and dampness of soil."

Janet goes on to write, "Finally the major portion of the land was purchased from the Charles and Mary Neish Heller farm, in the northwestern part of the city." Janet Heller Howell is the great granddaughter of Charles and Mary Neish Heller. Their farm house, built in 1840 would be moved from the farm, across Bancroft Road and is the large yellow home on the corner of Bancroft Road and Lena Place. In her article she broke down the land purchases as follows:

"The original purchases of land in 1858 included: Charles and Mary Heller, 12½ acres, $1,680; Frances and Isreal Coates, two areas each of 12½ acres, each for $1,687, Polly and Belorman Marsh, 12½ acres; then in succession came these purchases; 1874 Charles and Mary Heller, 32 and approximately ½ acres $32,565; 1892 Charles and Mary Heller, 17 and a fraction acres $1,700.20; 1899, Lerange Bancroft 73½ acres $11,000; 1920 Zera Compton, 10 acres, $4,000." She noted that except for the initial investment of funds, the land purchases have not cost the taxpayers any money.

The last purchase of land was in 1966 when 1½ acres were purchased from John and Dorothy Terris for $6,000.

After over a year's construction, at a cost of $17,000, a new mortuary chapel was opened at the cemetery in December of 1907.

The headline in the December 8 *Telegram* read, "It may be a pleasure to die just to have a chance to have the last rites observed in this artistic vestibule to the grave."

Photograph of Stephens Chapel by Diane Janowski.

Earlier in the week, on December 6, the *Star-Gazette* described the chapel, designed by architects Pierce and Bickford, as "the most beautiful chapel for religious purposes in the city...," paid for from the earnings of the cemetery alone. The paper reported the purpose of the new chapel was "to afford a beautiful house in which the dead may be given fitting burial services without cost and where all may be served alike...."

In 1960, the chapel, which had not been used for funerals in many years, was converted into offices and meeting room quarters. The Cemetery Commission office was relocated from city hall, and the cemetery superintendent moved his office from his home at the Walnut Street entrance to the renovated building. The commission paid the cost of $8,000 to $10,000 from its general fund.

Stay tuned for "the rest of the story" on page 91.

The Richardson tomb. Photo by Diane Janowski.

LANDLOCKED IN COMMITTEE—The "Mississippi," sternwheeler sought by Elmira and other communities, sits quietly at its Memphis mooring awaiting Congressional action. The nameplate on the front of the pilot house atop the Texas deck has been removed to a new flood control namesake vessel by Army Corps of Engineers, which owns the boat.

Image from the *Star-Gazette* dated January 4, 1962 page 23.

We Almost Had a Riverboat

By Diane Janowski

Back in 1962, a group of Elmirans wanted a riverboat for Eldridge Park. The group called themselves the "761 Committee." Their idea was to purchase an 1882 riverboat named the "Mississippi III." It had been refitted three times hence the "III" after its name. The ship was commissioned in 1927 as a high-water inspector between Cairo, Illinois and New Orleans. It was the most powerful Engineer Corps boat in the lower Mississippi valley. In 1946 it was reassigned as a work boat.

According to the January 4, 1962, *Star-Gazette*, the 761 Committee was headed by Stan Douglas and Mike Morgan. A financial arrangement was "in the works for the 220-foot vessel." Similar ships had been used on the Mississippi River for more than 100 years. The Army Corps of Engineers had offered several Texas stern-wheelers for sale and this was the last of the group. The ship had been out of commission at Memphis, Tennessee since its replacement with a new ship. Its nameplates and fittings had been moved to the new ship, but it still had "the air of its elegant past." Wall-to-wall carpeting, a grand lounge, a huge galley, heavy mahogany sideboard, and dining tables adorned the "Mississippi III."

The problem with the sale was the "Mississippi III" was awaiting dismantling and "honorable burial." Democrat Frank Smith, a representative from Mississippi, believed that the ship might be a nice showpiece for a museum or non-profit group. This is where Elmira caught wind of the idea. Hannibal, Missouri also wanted the ship as a restaurant or gambling ship.

The ship was valued at $322,000. Over the years, more than a million dollars had been spent on new boilers, a new cabin, a new hull, and other mechanical repairs.

It was hoped that Elmira might use it as a Mark Twain museum, commemorating Twain for spending his summers here and writing many books. Locals requested that the New York State Legislature back a special bill in Congress.

The plan was that the "Mississippi III" could be towed from Memphis up the Mississippi River to the Great Lakes, through the Erie Canal, the barge canal, and through Seneca Lake to Watkins Glen. There it could be dismantled and brought to Eldridge Lake for reassembly. Engineers believed that the ship was in good enough shape that the deck and walls could be left intact. The exterior needed paint, but the engines were working. It was considered a fine museum specimen.

One year later on January 3, 1963, a *Star-Gazette* headline read, "Elmira Won't Get Steamboat." The plan for our boat was scuttled after a man in St. Louis was the highest of twelve bidders. He offered $35,111 with hopes of turning it into a museum either in St. Louis or Hannibal. Our 761 Committee had bid $1.

Now, you all know I need the rest of the story, so I went looking for John C. Groffell, Jr. the man who bought the boat. Did it really become a museum in Hannibal? Well, his boat purchase made headlines in 48 newspapers all across the US.

In the Neosho, Missouri *Daily News* on Sept 11, 1964, the headline read, "Boat Docked at Hannibal now Tourist Mecca." Groffell did have the "Mississippi III" remodeled with a restaurant and "scale models and pictures of early Mississippi riverboats, replicas of guns, and illustrations of river hazards."

In 1965 the "Mississippi III" was sold and moved to St. Louis. It became the "Becky Thatcher" next to the "Tom Sawyer" moored near the Gateway Arch. The original "Becky Thatcher, an "entertainment boat" was smashed to bits when the river dropped and the crew had neglected to slacken the ropes. In 1975 the "Mississippi III" was purchased by the town of Marietta, Ohio for use as a restaurant/dinner theater. In 2010, the Pittsburg *Post-Gazette* reported that the ship was the victim of record snowfall and succumbed under the weight. The two top floors caused the 84-year-old boat to collapse.

St. Louis did replace the "Becky Thatcher/Mississippi III" with a new "Becky Thatcher."

Sources:

Star-Gazette (Elmira, New York) 04 Jan 1962, Thu Page 23
Star-Gazette Elmira, New York Thursday, January 03, 1963 - Page 13
https://www.riverfronttimes.com/newsblog/2010/02/24/rip-becky-thatcher-historic-steamboat-with-ties-to-st-louis-sinks-outside-pittsburgh
The Neosho *Daily News* (Neosho, Missouri) 11 Sep 1964, Fri Page 7
St. Louis *Post-Dispatch* (St. Louis, Missouri) 03 Sep 1961, Sun Page 63
Ibid 08 Dec 1967 page 12

The oldest graves in Woodlawn Cemetery were brought over from Wisner Cemetery in the 1850s. Photo by Diane Janowski.

Woodlawn Cemetery, Part Two

By James Hare

"Tread lightly—God is in this place,
This is His holy ground;
The glory from His radiant face
Shines o'er us all around;
Tread lightly e'en thou though Jesus child,
For often tiny feet
Pass o'er death's stream, so dark, so wild
The precious One to meet."

The above lines are the opening stanza of a poem written by an unnamed member of the Elmira College senior class for the dedication of Woodlawn Cemetery, October 9, 1858. According to the Elmira *Gazette*, the ceremonies for the dedication began Saturday the 9th at 10am in front of the court house on Lake Street. A procession was formed composed of marching units, a band from Williamsport, the Southern Tier Rifles, the Elmira Brass Band, and societies of Masons, Odd Fellows, village trustees, clergy and citizens. The paper noted that, "it was about the finest procession ever seen in Elmira."

At the "Baptist" graveyard the procession halted to add the remains of Colonel John Hendy to the march, to bear them to the new location at Woodlawn Cemetery. He had been disinterred from his burial place so that he would be the first burial in the new cemetery. With "martial music and impressive dignity," the procession continued.

Ceremonies at the cemetery included prayers, an original hymn composed by a member of the Elmira College senior class. The major address was given by the Rev. Dr. David Murdoch, pastor of the First Presbyterian Church. At the conclusion of the ceremonies, the remains of Col.

Hendy were re-interred at the new location marking the first burial for the new cemetery.

Once the village had decided to purchase land for a new burial ground, a plan needed to be made for the layout of the site. By the 1850's the "Rural Cemetery Movement" was underway across the country. As the Village of Elmira had grown, both the "Baptist" Cemetery, in what is now Wisner Park and the Second Street Cemetery were being surrounded by the growth of the community. The location of Woodlawn Cemetery was former farm land. Even Second Street Cemetery had been "rural" when opened. By the 1820's, after a wave of cholera, typhoid and yellow fever outbreaks in American cities, concern over the health risks of inner-city burials became widespread. This issue, plus overcrowding and rising land prices made the idea of a rural location attractive.

Based on English and French precedents, the American rural cemetery landscape was one of winding roads and picturesque vistas. The man that the village selected to design Woodlawn was Howard Daniels. According to former City Historian, and currently the President of the Friends of Woodlawn Cemetery, the Rev. John Humphries, Daniels was, "a noted landscape architect of the pre-Civil War era. A proponent of the rural garden cemetery movement, he studied in England and the United States and is considered one of 19th century America's most preeminent and prolific landscape architects. Woodlawn embodies the characteristics of a rural cemetery of the 1800's, and is the work of a master containing walks, lanes and roads arranged in a serpentine order, with numerous trees, plantings and shrubbery, all of which create an inviting park like ambiance... It is Daniels connection which has contributed to Elmira's Woodlawn Cemetery being accepted for inclusion at the National Cultural Landscape Foundation, as well as being listed on the National Register of Historic Places and more recently as a "Point of Interest."(designation as a Point of Interest is a way of publicly acknowledging a property's value to the community)

The Friends of Woodlawn Cemetery was incorporated in 2006 with the stated purpose to "save, restore and protect the historic aspects of the Woodlawn Cemetery." The organization received Internal Revenue

Stones in Woodlawn Cemetery. Photo by Diane Janowski.

Service 501 (c)(3) status in 2007 as a tax-exempt organization. Since that time, a number of projects have been undertaken. The Stephen's Memorial has been restored, sign posts have been placed a the avenues of the historic part of the cemetery, the exterior fencing has been painted and in some places replaced with the Friends covering the cost.

For twelve years, cooperating with the Elmira Little Theater and the Chemung County Historical Society, the Friends have hosted Ghost Night at the cemetery. During the two evenings in October "residents" of the cemetery and indeed historic figures from our past are portrayed and their stories are told.

Stay tuned for part three on page 101.

Friends have established a website at
www.FriendsOfWoodlawnElmira.org

Stones in Woodlawn Cemetery. Photo by Diane Janowski.

A Special Visit From Three Celebrities

by Diane Janowski

What do General MacArthur, Aunt Jemima, and Miss Brazil 1954 have in common? Well, in 1954, within seven days, you could have shaken hands with all three celebrities right here in Elmira.

In 1954, the Remington-Rand plant on South Main Street was the largest typewriter factory in the world. The company was celebrating the assembly of the 15-millionth typewriter made in Elmira. On September 8, General Douglas MacArthur, war hero, and chairperson of the Board of Rand, was the honored guest of Rand's "Community Day."

Mac Arthur's plane arrived at the Chemung County airport at 9:25 AM. A party of Elmira's leading citizens, including Mayor Emory Strachen, met the flight with a police escort and accompanied MacArthur to the Rand plant for a tour and a ceremony. It was his first time in Elmira.

The smiling faces of Rand employees and the smell of fresh flower bouquets that adorned the factory greeted MacArthur. At the ceremony, he congratulated the workers on their job performances.

MacArthur and the mayor's hungry group then proceeded to the Mark Twain Hotel for a delicious luncheon for 450 guests at 12:15 PM. One of the guests was Miss Brazil 1954, also known as Martha Rocha. The *Star-Gazette* reported that she was wearing a "striking brown gown and hat that set off her brownish hair and attractive eyes." Upon meeting Miss Brazil 1954, MacArthur replied, "This is very pleasant, indeed." In the next day's *Star-Gazette,* reporter Jim Morse said he was a little surprised that Miss Brazil (Brazil being a coffee nation) turned down coffee and opted for milk. Miss Rocha was runner-up for Miss Universe. She did not speak English but did say, "I think you are all wonderful." Miss Rocha received a gift on behalf of Brazil – a replica of the 15-millionth typewriter.

FIFTEEN MILLIONTH TYPEWRITER. James H. Rand, president of Remington Rand and General MacArthur, chairman of the company's board, stand beside a table on which rests a historic machine. It is the 15 millionth manufactured by the company since 1873. Rand told MacArthur that 15 million more could be made in a tenth of the time with present-day manufacturing capacity.

The 15-millionth typewriter from Remington-Rand. Image from the *Star-Gazette* Sept. 9, 1954 page 23

Another "guest" at the dinner was Rand's 15-millionth typewriter. It had rolled off the production line shortly before noon that day. It was presented to the City of Elmira.

Elmira was very generous with gifts to General MacArthur. He received a gift of some Steuben glassware, an ashtray, and a monogrammed cigarette box. He commented that he had enjoyed his time in Elmira.

At 2:00 PM, a motorcade of open cars took the General and a small group on a tour of the city. The group circled the downtown area, and then stopped at Elmira College, where MacArthur presented them with an early Model One Remington typewriter (the one that is in Mark Twain's study).

Following the presentation, MacArthur left for the airport and departed at 3:05 PM aboard an American Airlines' flight.

BRAZILIAN GUESTS—William J. Vickery, manager of the Elmira plant of Remington Rand, chats with two guests who arrived Wednesday night for ceremonies at the plant and Community Day activities. From left are: Vickery, Miss Martha Rocha, "Miss Brazil of 1954," and Dr. Hugo Gouthier, consul-general of Brazil in New York City.

From the *Star-Gazette* Sept 9, 1954 page 20.

GREETING THE VISITOR—Two-year-old Bradley Buell (left) of 94 Redfield Dr., and Cheryl McLane, 4, of 750 Larchmont Rd., were among the estimated 500 persons who greeted Aunt Jemima yesterday morning when she arrived for the community pancake supper slated Thursday from 11 a. m to 8 p. m. at the State Armory. Aunt Jemima came by helicopter (inset) at the new Sears Roebuck and Co. parking lot on N. Main St. to attend the party being cosponsored by the Exchange Club and the Junior Association of Commerce.

Aunt Jemima arrived in Elmira on a helicopter.
Star-Gazette March 2, 1955 page 14.

On September 15, 1954 Aunt Jemima, the well-known pancake expert, was the guest of the Walnut Food Store on Walnut Street. I don't know if she was Ethel Ernestine Harper or another traveling Aunt Jemima, as I could not find mention of her true identity. Miss Harper was the second Aunt Jemima and the "basis for the image." Aunt Jemima was here for two days to "make and serve her delicious pancakes with the ever popular 'Vermont Maid Syrup.'" Then, she pointed out "how easy it was, and how little it cost to keep a family's appetite happy with frequent pancake feasts." Aunt Jemima also arrived in Elmira in 1955 via a helicopter that landed in the new Sears parking lot on North Main Street. She was also a guest of Elmira College in 1956 while in town to host a "Pancake Party" at the Armory. About 9,000 guests were expected. Only 1,000 could be fed at one sitting. Twenty griddles were set up for the hungry crowd. Included in the 50¢ meal were sausages, coffee, milk, and all kinds of pancake condiments.

The March 22 Elmira *Advertiser* reported that "Each housewife will receive a box of pancake flour as she leaves." Proceeds went to the Boy Scouts for the improvement of Rorick's Glen.

Hungry Elmirans consumed 4,000 pounds of pancakes, 300 pounds of sausages, 30 pounds of butter, 125 cases of maple syrup, and immeasurable amounts of coffee and milk that day. During the peak times, double lines stretched from the Armory to Baldwin Street and waited twenty minutes to be seated.

Sources:

Star-Gazette (Elmira, New York), Sept 8 and 9, 1954.

Star-Gazette (Elmira, New York) Sept 9, 1954 Page 20

The mausoleum at Woodlawn Cemetery. Photo by Diane Janowski.

Woodlawn Cemetery, Part Three

By James Hare

In 2018, Woodlawn Cemetery has well over 60,000 burial sites.

The cemetery reflects the history of our community. Originally, the "avenues were named after trees; Walnut, Tulip, Hickory, Linden, Elm, Sycamore (The Friends of Woodlawn have supplied granite signposts to designate the avenues). There are eleven mausoleums owned by individual families, some now abandoned," according to Janet Heller Howell in the June 1983 edition of the Chemung County Historical Society's *Journal*. The largest mausoleum was built in 1912, and had 370 crypts. The last burial was in 1980. Some bodies have been removed and it has fallen under the care of the city as no descendants can be located to take responsibility.

In her article, Janet Heller Howell, great granddaughter of the family who sold the property to the Village of Elmira for the cemetery, describes many of Woodlawn's "works of art." Some are: the "Eldridge-Reynolds-Stancliff plot fronted by four carved statues." The twelve foot high Hall marker, the Diven family plot marked by stone steps and carries a quotation from Saint John the Baptist and the beautiful marker of Ida May Seeley Davies. She also noted the Celtic cross monument marking the grave of Thomas A. Pagett.

As you enter the cemetery at the Walnut Street gate, adjacent to the superintendent's cottage is the Stephens Memorial. Behind the cottage and chapel are about eighty-five graves containing the bodies removed from the old Main Street "Baptist" Cemetery. The chapel was built by Margaret Stephens in 1896 as a memorial to her family with "free use" given to the people of Elmira to hold services there. Located in front of the chapel is a statue of a Grecian goddess bearing the inscription "in memory of my darling sister, Tut." The Stephens family is encrypted in the building undercroft. Restoration of this chapel has been a major project for the Friends of Woodlawn Cemetery.

In the southeast corner of the cemetery, along Davis Street, is a Jewish section assembled by the Sons of Abraham. The Sons were formed in 1886 as a charitable organization to provide for funerals for Jews of German descent who did not have the means. In 1891, they built a stucco chapel for prayer services before committal to the grave. Because of vandalism, the chapel was razed in 1945 and the gate at that location was sealed off. Over time the Sons of Abraham has evolved into the Cemetery Committee of Congregation Kol Ami which oversees the rituals of Jewish burials.

A little north of the Sons of Abraham plot is a huge rock located below Mark Twain's grave. It marks the final resting place of George and Crete McCann, early settlers of Elmira. Apparently the boulder was hauled from the east side of the Chemung Canal over a specially built bridge by several teams of oxen. Likenesses of the McCann's are on a bronze plaque attached to the boulder.

Not far from the McCann site, up the hill from the Davis Street gate is Smokey. Before the city paid fire department was established in 1878, bucket brigades of volunteers fought fires in Elmira and insurance companies hired some fire companies to protect certain buildings. Different companies each had their own territories in the city's neighborhoods. In 1903, the Firemen's Monument was dedicated to the memory of the volunteer fire companies. Martha Horton, Vice-President of the Friends of Woodlawn, wrote in the September, 2008 edition of the Chemung County Historical *Journal* that, "the famed fireman statue was even "kidnapped" from its base in 1975 by a gang of antiques thieves. It was happily recovered with the help of local FBI agent Robert Bucher from an antique shop in New England...." On June 14, 2008 "Smokey" was re-dedicated. Working with the late Elmira firefighter Greg Dunn, the Friends of Woodlawn contributed $2,250 toward the restoration project.

Down the lane from the Firemen's Monument is the Hendy Plot, marking the site of Colonel John Hendy, the first person to be interred at Woodlawn on October 9, 1858.

On Saturday, May 16, 1936, the Elks Memorial Marker was dedicated in the presence of national and state officers and many members. The marker identifies the plot known as Elks Rest. According to Supreme Court Justice of New York, James T. Hallinan, grand exalted ruler of the orders: "The Elks Rest will ever remind us that we are members of an order that believes in a Supreme Being, and is ever ready to defend the flag and give service to all. Membership in the Benevolent and Protective Order of Elks is the best asset America has against Communism and other isms."

Within the bounds of Woodlawn Cemetery are the famous, the not so famous and perhaps some scoundrels. Twelve members of the Unites States House of Representatives are at rest there. Two governors, Lucius Robinson, Governor of New York 1877-79 and Alexander W. Randall, Governor of Wisconsin 1858-62 and United States Postmaster General 1866-69.

Veterans have not been forgotten at the city's Woodlawn Cemetery. In March of 1945 a six ton boulder was placed at the approach to the Walnut Street gate to be dedicated to the veterans of all wars. The Chemung County Veteran Council sponsored the memorial with Harry Butters, Clair H. Horton and Frank T. Ketter of that organization pictured on the bronze plaque.

In the 160 years of Woodlawn Cemetery, the community has changed, the architecture and nature of burial and placement of remains has changed. It has been reported that over 50% of people are now choosing to be cremated instead of traditional burial. To respond to that need, the Friends of Woodlawn have purchased a columbarium and is working with the cemetery commission to create a Cremation Garden.

In one of his stories, the French writer Albert Camus illuminated the human condition in two words that sound almost identical: solitaire and solidaire—"apart" and "part of." As a solitary being each of us merits a separate grave; as members of a group, we are buried together. Cemeteries are an outgrowth of communities that create them, and they often become focal points for family, religious, ethnic, regional or national celebration, that simultaneously honor the dead and enhance a sense of group identity among the living.

A scene at the Senators' Cottage. My aunt Anna Janowski Roemelt is the woman standing on the right. Circa 1915. Photo courtesy of author

Oh, Those Summer Nights

by Diane Janowski

Believe it or not, living in Elmira was so stressful in the olden days that many Elmirans either owned or rented cottages along the Chemung River as far up stream as Fitch's Bridge and downstream too, as far as the Katy-did Cottage at Katy-did Curve. Family and club cottages provided weekend, holiday, and vacation retreats from the cares and worries of living in Elmira.

Sometimes clubs held outings or dinners at their own cottages. In the days before automobiles, folks rode the streetcar as far as it would go then walked the rest of the way.

Some of the cottage names were Bohemia-on-the-Chemung, Arcadia-on-the-Chemung, Happy Thought, Senator's, Crickett, Pine Cliff Club, Hiawatha Cottage-on-the-Chemung, Ave-Lacy, and Never-Worry. Finding their present locations proved difficult to me as they didn't really have addresses.

The society pages of old newspapers were full of names of folks who were having wonderful times fishing, boating and swimming in the river. Some cottages had electricity and telephones, some were rustic. Most were furnished with a boat and canoe, and a fireplace.

The *Star-Gazette* on Sept 14, 1896 reported, "The French and Myers campers at Zimmerman's cottage near Baden-Baden down the river were besieged by visitors from the city yesterday and the cooking over the old-fashioned fireplace was a great success." Baden-Baden was a questionable cottage. In the days of Prohibition, there was a good possibility that alcohol was "occasionally" served. Baden-Baden was located "on the north bank of the Chemung River off Rt. 17 about three miles east of the Fort Reed Bridge." Fort Reed Bridge was where the on ramp to I-86 at the end of East Water Street over Newtown Creek is today.

On July 7, 1909 the *Star-Gazette* said, "Thomas and Nellie Horigan are spending a week at the Rest-a-While cottage on the Chemung."

The same day a snippet said, "The following have returned from a pleasing outing at the Tory Meadow Cottage on the Chemung. The Misses Mame Kane, Nellie Dougherty, Josephine McInerney, Margaret Costello, and the Messrs. Michael and Thomas McInerney, James McCrone and Mr. and Mrs John McInerney, and son Gerald.

On July 31, 1909 the *Star-Gazette* said "The following are enjoying an outing at the Eggert Cottage, Arcadia-on-the-Chemung River: Mrs. Anna Nolan and daughters Anna and Bessie; Miss Marie O'Shea, Mrs. M. Roache, Joseph and Thomas Nolan. Another mention on August 16, 1913 said, "Mr. and Mrs. John Pack and family are spending some time at Mountain View Cottage-on-the-Chemung."

On October 3, 1918 the *Star-Gazette* reported "A toothsome dinner of broiled lake trout was served at Katy-Did Cottage-near-Chemung to which the guests motored. Three in the party expect to be called for military service soon." Katy-Did Cottage was "situated twelve miles east of Elmira.

Picnic parties along the river sometimes turned dangerous. The Star-Gazette on Aug 4, 1920 reported a drowning accident while swimming at Katy-Did Cottage. It involved a young couple - Henry Ziegler of Kinyon Street, and his friend Beatrice French of Junction Street. Henry was swept away in the current and drowned. Beatrice was rescued. There were numerous accounts of other drownings while at cottage retreats.

I found a 1919 snippet in the socials that included both of my grandparents along with 8 other young people (boys and girls) and 2 matronly chaperones, of course, at the Sun-Shine Cottage. This mention was well before my grandparents were married. I am guessing this was a church-related retreat as the other names do come from my family church. They married seven years later. Maybe this trip started it all? My church did have a Sunshine Circle, also known as their sewing club.

These summer cottages held many parties – apparently with a lot of room. A clipping from the August 31, 1921 *Star-Gazette* says "Miss Nina Spencer entertained 20 couples at Sun-Shine Cottage Tuesday evening. Cards and dancing were enjoyed throughout the evening and a picnic supper was enjoyed."

Happy Thought Cottage in 1958. Photo in *Star-Gazette* June 22, 1958 page 17.

Locations for these cottages have been hard to track down. The Senators' Cottage was "up the river above the old Mountain House - farther west on the highway to the rear and south of the Harris Hill Inn." Directions to a big party there included "A carryall will meet streetcars at the end of the West Water Street line and carry the pleasure seekers to the Cottage, over the picturesque ride through the narrows. Dinner will be served at 4 o'clock, and will include all of the delicacies of the season, with broilers as the main dish."

My Aunt Anna Janowski Roemelt was a frequent guest at the Senators' Cottage. I have her photos of happy times there.

Lone Pine Cottage was on the top of Mt. Zoar above Rorick's Glen. Canoe Camp was on an island opposite Rorick's Glen. Recreation Club Cottage was "opposite Bohemia on the south shore."

Some of you may remember Stanley Woods in Golden Glow. Bohemia-on-the-Chemung and Happy Thought were "just west of Fitch's Bridge at the eastern end of a private cottage group."

Pine Cliff Cottage was "just west of Happy Thought." The directions to Pine Cliff included, "by streetcar as far as Clark's Glen and walking the remainder of the way." This was a dirty affair as the road was usually muddy or dusty. Far View Cottage was a "retreat for 15 young Elmira bachelors" – that they built themselves. The Hard-Boiled Egg Club had a cottage nearby with two platforms overlooking the river, and a bathing house.

On August 4, 1934 classified ads listed four rentable cottages in the Demarest Parkway area for $18 a week or by the day.

The last mention I found for Katy-Did Cottage was in 1939. After the 1946 flood, the Army Corps changed the access to the river with the additions of bigger and higher levees.

By the 1950s many cottages had been refurbished into year-round living spaces. The 1972 flood eliminated many of the former cottages along the river.

PROTECT YOUR CHILD AGAINST RUBELLA

A new vaccine is available for Rubella (three-day measles). New York State Law requires that your child be vaccinated for Rubella.

One Rubella vaccination is recommended for all children ages one through ten years.

If your child is allergic to rabbits, chickens, eggs or feathers, approval must be obtained from your family physician before immunization will be given.

A small percentage of the children may experience some joint aches and pains.

Yes, I want my child to receive the Rubella Vaccine in this clinic.

BRING THIS FORM WITH YOUR CHILD TO THE CLINICS TO BE HELD SUNDAY, OCTOBER 18 FROM NOON TO 4 P.M. AT THE BIG FLATS AND VAN ETTEN TOWN HALLS, MILLPORT FIRE HOUSE AND THE 4-H BUILDING AT THE CHEMUNG COUNTY FAIR GROUNDS.

Child's Name ________ ________ Age ______ Birth Date ____ Sex ____

Address

Is your child: 1. Allergic? Yes ________ No ________

If so, to what

2. Taking any drugs or medicine regularly?

Yes ________ No ______

If so, what ____________

3. YOUR CHILD SHOULD NOT HAVE RECEIVED ORAL POLIO, SMALLPOX OR REGULAR MEASLES VACCINE SINCE SEPT. 18, 1970

Date ______________ ______________________

Parent or Guardian Signature

From the *Star-Gazette*. October 19, 1970 Page 8

Measles and Other Epidemics

By Diane Janowski

My father tells the story that when I was five I got a measles shot, yet a week later I had a bad case of measles. I don't remember those measles, but I do remember having chicken pox a year later when my brother and I both had it at the same time.

This got me thinking about diseases and in looking for recorded instances of epidemics in our area I found many listed. Cholera, smallpox, measles, typhoid, and polio were mentioned the most. Cholera and typhoid come from water and food supplies. Smallpox, measles and polio come from personal contact.

In July 1849, Millport had a cholera epidemic that killed as many as 375, depending on the source, mostly Irish laborers who were working on the Northern Central railroad. The New York *Evening Post* on August 1, 1849 mentioned that two residents - including the head of the Millport board of health died. "In many cases the attack was so sudden and violent that death resulted in three or four hours," according to historian Ausburn Towner. Laborers left in droves. This epidemic was all over New York State.

In the winter of 1864-65, smallpox epidemic at the Elmira Prison Camp claimed 300 lives within the camp.

Reports from the Elmira *Daily Gazette* included:

"Measles are prevalent at Pine Valley," on May 5, 1891.
"Arnot [PA] has over 400 cases and the doctors of that place are overworked," on April 21, 1891.
"Measles are raging at Big Flats. Ten cases are reported," on May 21, 1891.

A *Daily Gazette* headline on December 31, 1894 said "Quite an Epidemic." "A prominent physician" said that there were many cases of typhoid fever, but that, in his opinion, many of those were [really] malaria, which contains many of the same symptoms."

The Buffalo *Commercial* on January 15, 1895 reported, "They are having a mild epidemic of typhoid in Elmira."

In 1896, a typhoid outbreak lasted more than three months. It was believed that the city water was the culprit. More than 275 cases. The organist of the Park Church moved to Watkins Glen for the duration seeking "a more healthful locality."

On July 18, 1896 a *Daily Gazette* headline read "UNFIT FOR USE" after reservoir water samples taken by local health officer W. C. Wey and sent to Professor E. M. Chamot, a chemical analyst at Cornell University. Chamot's conclusion proved that our water was "too high in organic matter and microorganisms to be fit for drinking purposes." He said the samples seemed to be "close to stagnant water. I believe the water is unfit for drinking." He advised that water be boiled for at least thirty minutes, but 2 or 3 hours would be better.

The October 27, 1899, Elmira *Gazette* reported an epidemic of typhoid started by contaminated milk supplied by a farmer with a case of typhoid. Six cases were reported along the milkman's route. It was believed that the cans had been washed with contaminated water.

Between February and June 1913, a smallpox epidemic hit Elmira. Forty residents contracted it. "Vaccinations prevented a spread of the disease."

On January 6, 1916 the *Star-Gazette* reported "Elmira Physicians Swamped with Calls" of pneumonia. It was particularly prevalent amongst Elmirans who recently returned from Chicago, Detroit, Philadelphia, and Pittsburg. Doctors said to "avoid overheated and overcrowded places. Dress warmly when out in the cold. Avoid alcohol. Be sure to get plenty of rest and fresh air.

In 1918, the Spanish Influenza epidemic killed 189 Chemung Countians – 134 in Elmira alone. The epidemic lasted from about October 11 until after Christmas that year. Schools and churches closed, people avoided going to work. St. Joseph's and the Arnot-Ogden hospitals were overwhelmed and the Gotham Hotel was converted into a hospital. It lasted in Elmira for over a year and a half.

On March 23, 1931, Elmira city health officer Dr. Reeve B. Howland said "he expects a cycle that brings a measles epidemic – he asserted that the cycle comes every three years." He recommended to isolate the first cases and to give them plenty of fresh air.

On December 7, 1934 a *Star-Gazette* headline read "Schools Report Drop in Measles Epidemic: 177 cases on record." This was Elmira's worst measles outbreak to date. In Elmira, 784 school children had it on one particular day. School superintendent Harvey Hutchinson estimated that the epidemic cost Elmira around $5000 in lost state aid.

In 1944 a polio, or infantile paralysis, epidemic hit Elmira between June and December, with 313 cases with 10 deaths reported. In a 48-hour interval 11 new cases were reported. 53 were treated at the Arnot Ogden and 21 were treated at St. Joseph's – must be that the rest recuperated at home. Street addresses of patients included Gaines, Luce, Davis, Robert, Baldwin, Miller, Upper Oakwood, Walnut, Locust Streets, Delaware Avenue, and Broadway. In July 1944 Board of Health banned children "16 and under"

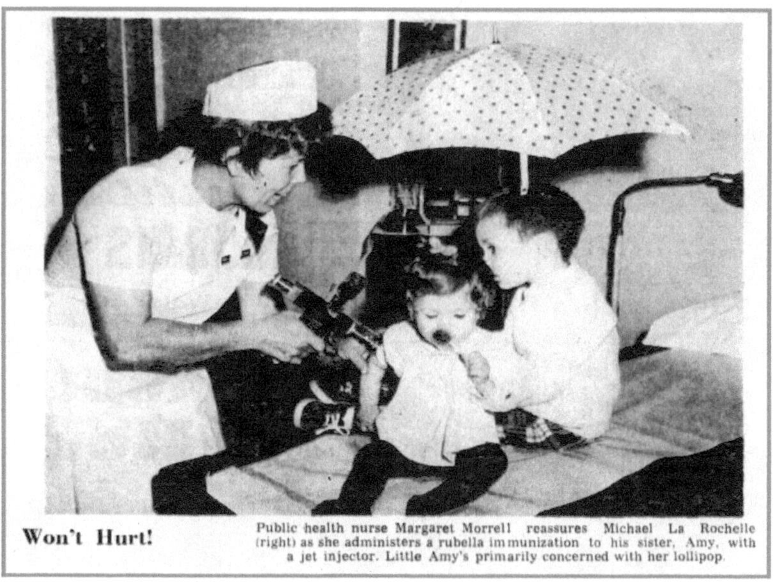

Won't Hurt! Public health nurse Margaret Morrell reassures Michael La Rochelle (right) as she administers a rubella immunization to his sister, Amy, with a jet injector. Little Amy's primarily concerned with her lollipop.

From the *Star-Gazette*. October 15, 1970 Page 17

from Dunn Field, all city parks, theaters, and even the Chemung County Fair.

Another polio outbreak hit Elmira in 1953. Forty cases by July 18. Officials struggled because the outside temp was 98° and Elmirans usually cooled off at Brand Park pool. Luckily, it was decided that the pool remain open because of its chlorine content.

In 1946 another measles epidemic with 1600 cases.

In 1952, measles came again with 2,352 cases.

A vaccine for measles was introduced in 1963 and cases worldwide dropped sharply.

My brother says he remembers being in a long line of children at a vaccination clinic at the Chemung County fairgrounds in the early 1970s. He was right October 17, 1970 – I found the form for rubella (German measles) vaccine while doing this research. A medical team using "jet injector guns" was able to "painlessly vaccinate over 400 children an hour."

Sources:

Star-Gazette (Elmira, New York) 19 Jul 1944, Wed Page 5

The Evening Post (New York, New York) 01 Aug 1849, Wed Page 2

Sgro Brothers

by James Hare

"Dom Sgro remembers everything about playing the harmonica on the 'Ed Sullivan Show.'

He remembers the date, September 19, 1954. He remembers how kind Ed Sullivan was. And he remembers why he missed a note playing 'The St. Louis Blues.'"

A publicity photo supplied by the Sgro Brothers.

We were playing, and I looked out at the audience, and there she was, staring at me. I forgot about the forty million people watching TV. I missed a note, because, my God, she was looking directly at me.

'She' was Gina Lollobrigida, the beautiful Italian actress. She thrilled him by chatting with him in Italian after the performance."

John Cleary reported this story for the *Star-Gazette* on November 11, 2003 as the Sgro Brothers, Dom and Tony, were preparing to perform with Ed Sullivan impersonator Will Jordan in a recreation of the Ed Sullivan Show. Ed had died in 1974.

In the sixty five years since that appearance with Ed Sullivan, the Sgro Brothers have not missed a beat, and are still going strong. Dom, at age 87, and Tony at 85 are preparing to appear at the Upper Ohio Valley Italian Festival in July at Wheeling, West. Virginia. They will be performing the opening for Bill Haley and the Comets of 'Rock Around the Clock' fame. Of course Bill died in 1981 so this group is a recreation.

The Festival is important to the Sgro Brothers because in 2006, they were inducted into the Lou Holtz Upper Ohio Valley Hall of Fame. The Hall was created to honor Lou Holtz, but has a dual purpose of "recognizing residents and natives of the Upper Ohio Valley in all fields of endeavor who can serve as inspirational role models for the region's young people." The Sgro Brothers were born in the region.

The brothers are proud of their Italian heritage. Their father Frank, and mother Felicia married in Calabria, Italy in 1919. Frank then came to the United States seeking a job and to establish residency leaving Felicia in Italy.

Over the next ten years he traveled back and forth to Italy fathering Ralph, Peter and Josephine. Finally, in 1930, he was able to bring the entire family to the United States, settling in Wellsville, Ohio. Dom appeared in 1932, with Tony showing up in 1934. Josephine, at 98, still resides in Wellsville.

Frank had a great love for music and played the violin, mandolin and guitar. One Christmas, when Dom was six and Tony four, Frank gave each of them a harmonica as a gift. Self-taught, and eighty years later they love their harmonicas. According to Tony, at Dom's suggestion, he plays the "larger and more expensive" chord harmonica, while Dom plays the smaller chromatic melody harmonica. Dom offers as one reason for their longevity is that in the cardiovascular world the blowing and drawing make the harmonica a most effective instrument.

Their career began while in high school in Wellsville. They became "stage struck" while performing in an Easter Pageant and inspired when they saw the famous "Borrah Minevitch Harmonica Rascals," in the movies. Dom and Tony competed in talent shows eventually being noted by agents and getting booked in the Pittsburgh, Cleveland, Akron area. Radio station WOHL of East Liverpool, Ohio invited them to perform a weekly Monday night radio show and they had their own Italian radio show every Sunday morning in Alliance, Ohio, all this while still teenagers.

After Tony graduated from high school, he and Dom joined the Marine Air Reserve. With the advent of the Korean War, Dom got his draft notice. He and Tony decided to enlist in the Marine Corps in hopes of keeping together. Indeed they were kept together in Special Services. They were known as the Marine Corp's Own Harmaniacs.

Teaming up with Igor "Eddie" Sedor, a high school friend, they traveled the country leading to the 1954 appearance with Ed Sullivan.

After leaving the Marines in 1955, Dom and Tony worked in New York City. In 1956, they joined "little" Johnny Puleo's Harmonica Gang and traveled the world. Tony recalls playing the London Palladium for sixteen weeks and having to back off the stage after performing for the Queen. Dom remembers being kicked by "little" Johnny as part of the act. They played with Herb Shriner, did TV shows and recorded for Columbia Records.

While in New York they were introduced to Lucy and Angela DiNardo, two sisters from Hornell, New York working in the city. Tony and Lucy married in 1957, Dom and Angela in 1958. Dom and Angela had three daughters and eleven grandchildren. Sadly, Lucy died in 1987, and Angela in 2018. Tony remarried with Dorothy Demyan in 2002. She and her first husband had been Sgro Brothers fans. After his death in 1994, Dorothy, on a "ladies night out" at the Clemens Center to see the Lettermen, and ran into Tony. Using his "connections" to get an autograph, she and Tony became a couple and married in 2002.

The Sgro families settled in Elmira in 1961. New York City was expensive, Hornell a bit isolated and Elmira had an airport. While still doing some traveling to perform, Tony noted that they "could not make a full time living playing strictly music in the Elmira area. In 1967, they purchased the former Melody Gardens at 115 Westside Avenue and opened their own restaurant. Over the next ten years the likes of George Jessel, George Goble, Frank Fontaine (Crazy Guggenheim), Donald O'Connor and many other stars joined the Sgros at their restaurant. In 1974, the Sgro Brothers appeared at the Grand Old Opry. Dom said they were the "first Italian hillbillies" to perform there. Their sponsor was Odom Sausage and U.S. Borax. In 1977, as the Sgros "were starting to make their move," the restaurant was sold.

To visit with the Sgro Brothers is to be impressed with their vitality, enthusiasm, love of music and entertaining. They have performed with Dean Martin at his first solo performance after breaking up with Jerry Lewis, seven times with Perry Como, Tennessee Ernie Ford, Gabby Hayes just to name a few. A favorite recollection for Tony is appearing with Frank Sinatra and Dom tells of playing at the White House and meeting President George W. Bush in 2004.

Kelli L. Huggins in her book, *Curiosities of Elmira,* wrote "there have been many famous Elmirans, even if their names are no longer remembered today… Some performers traveled widely, showcasing their talents…." The Sgro Brothers have performed in London, Havana, Las Vegas and Brand Park. They booked a performance at Eldridge Park as we talked. Then before I left the interview, they asked what type of music do I like. I said Gospel and they played "Amazing Grace."

In a 2008 article for *Mountain Home* magazine, local author Martha Horton identified five Sgro Brothers "Firsts"

1st Harmonica duo to play the White House
1st Harmonica duo to play the Grand Old Opry
1st Harmonica duo to play Avery Fisher Hall at Lincoln Center, NYC
1st Harmonica duo ever to be recorded in stereo (1957)
1st Harmonica duo to receive a Lifetime Achievement Award from the worldwide Society for the Preservation and Advancement of the Harmonica

About the authors and this book series....

Diane Janowski is the current Elmira City historian. She is also the editor of *New York History Review,* and was formerly the editor of the *Chemung Historical Journal.*

She has written many books about Elmira and Chemung County history, and co-authored the book *Images of America, The Chemung Valley* with Allen C. Smith.

James Hare is a retired teacher of American History and Government from the Elmira City School District. He is also a former mayor and councilman for the City of Elmira.

He co-authored the book *Images of America, Elmira* with former county historian J. Arthur Kieffer.

Hare and Janowski are freelance writers for the Elmira *Star-Gazette.* Since 2014, they each write monthly articles on the history of the city of Elmira, New York. This book is a selection of their articles.

Be sure to look for our other books!

TRUE STORIES

of Elmira, New York

Volumes 1 , 2 , and 3

By Diane Janowski & James Hare

www.ingramcontent.com/pod-product-compliance
Lightning Source LLC
LaVergne TN
LVHW091009080826
845145LV00003B/1191

* 9 7 8 1 9 5 0 8 2 2 0 6 5 *